IGNITION
Answer Your Calling

Dr. Farookh Sensei
with Nasreen Variyawa

www.farookhsensei.com

Foreword by Ms. Serena Brown Travis

The daughter of legendary Motivational Speaker Les Brown and the President & CEO of Les Brown Unlimited.

Serena Brown Travis

When someone shouts our name, we curiously turn to them and answer "Yes?" When our phone rings, we quickly retrieve it, examine the numbers and answer, "Hello?" But when there is a calling on our lives, many times it is difficult to immediately answer and pursue the purpose designed for us. *Why?*

Carrying a calling with a great mission can feel like a burden as one usually feels ill-equipped, unprepared, like a fish out of water. Avoiding a divine calling or push to move in a foreign direction carries great consequences, while, leading a life of mediocrity and normalcy seems far more attractive than stretching your wings, growing in adversity, and tackling a new project to achieve new goals.

If you have run from your calling, do not fret, you are in good company. Look at Moses who ran from the task of freeing his people from bondage. Moses ran into the wilderness for over 40 years to avoid his destiny, yet, it was only Moses who could fearlessly declare *"Let my people go!"*

Reader, where are you? Really, look around you. Are you stuck? Are your stumbling blocks really your step stools to pick yourself up? They usually are, but the challenge of picking yourself up, dusting yourself off, and moving forward seems too hard of a burden to bear. Are you tired of running from your destiny yet?

IGNITION Answer Your Calling by Dr. Farookh Sensei is your solution to finding courage, strength, and comfort in saying "Yes" to the assignment on your life. The brilliant authors throughout this book give their personal accounts of the joys and challenges of answering the calling. This book is a near blueprint for how to step into the realm of the unknown and get clear on stepping into your destiny.

I remember I recently answered a calling on my life that I had been running from for over 15 years. I told a dear friend, "I would be okay if God just told me what he wanted to do with my life. Then, this call thing would feel better." My friend laughed and quickly said, "If God told you what he wanted to do, you would manipulate the process and do the opposite."

Can I gently suggest to you, stop manipulating the process? Let's be honest, you have felt the calling on your life and have had visions for your success and greatness. *Answer Your Calling*!

The World is Waiting on Your Gift,

Serena Brown Travis
The Pulpit Chic

Hello & Welcome

IGNITION - "Answer your calling" is a collection of true stories written by 27 successful authors, mentors and coaches who appeared on my chat show – Ignition.

The purpose of this book is to inspire readers to take massive action to transform their lives, bring change to their communities and inspire others to do the same. The authors in this book selflessly talk about themselves, their experiences and even give advice to others wanting to do the same as them.

This book takes me to a time when all I knew was that I had it in me to succeed and that I had a calling but didn't know how I was going to get there. I didn't have anyone to guide me and so I can imagine how aspiring leaders wanting to make a breakthrough would feel when they have no real point of reference.

The birth of my chat show was accidental. Nasreen Variyawa, a mentee on mine who had written her 2nd book "Ignite the Champion within and Inspire others to begin" asked me to interview her about the book. We launched the video on her fan page to give the book exposure and suddenly had many enquiries from aspiring authors wanting to be interviewed by me. Ignition was born about a month later. I learnt that sometimes the best ideas come quite by accident and certainly whilst helping others to achieve their goals and dreams - this is the power of caring and sharing.

Ignition is a part of our legacy and we are humbled to leave it behind for anyone who will read it and use it to make the world a better place to live.

Dr. Farookh Sensei

Dedication To My Teachers

Late Shihan Bonnie Roberts (8th Dan Black Belt)

Soke Hirokazu Kanazawa (Karate Legend 10th Dan Black Belt)

Les Brown (No. 1 Motivational Guru in the World)

Dr. John Maxwell (No. 1 Leadership Guru in the World)

Acknowledgement

"Catch a falling star and put it in your pocket, never let it fade away. Catch a falling star and put it in your pocket, save it for a rainy day..." **Paul Vance and Lee Pockriss**

Well, I have been catching stars all summer. They have all descended on me with magnificent stories, experiences and anecdotes that I literally have put into my pocket.

No words to thank Ms. Serena Brown Travis, the daughter of Mr. Les Brown and the President & CEO of Les Brown Unlimited for writing a wonderful foreword for this book.

Thanks to the founder & CEO of the ATS Jr, Companies and one of the top 101Global trainer and thought leader Antonio T. Smith Jr, for personally supporting us in the finishing of this book.

Thanks to every author for their contribution to this wonderful book. Without you this book would have never born. I am so pleased to have worked with all of you and I am so pleased to know all of you.

Thanks to Dr. Farookh Sensei for giving me the opportunity to work with all the authors and for holding true the leadership principle of empowerment. I am humbled and grateful.

Keep smiling, keep shining, and keep rising

Nasreen Variyawa
Editor in C1hief

27 Inspiring Stories

IGNITION 1

You Are The Entire Ocean, In A Drop

Antonio T. Smith Jr.

Rumi once said, "You are not a drop in the ocean, you are an entire ocean, in a drop." It is with this fundamental understanding that I have made a difference the world. I have convinced millions of people that we are all connected and that there is only one of us in the room. What is more beautiful than a stadium filled with people coming to the understanding that all of us are connected, and that all of us are one. I have become the champion of connection. I connect people where there was once disconnection.

However, my life did not begin this way. I was actually homeless from six to eighteen years of age. My parents gave me up and left me for dead and life became a disaster. There I was, less than 24 kilograms (about 54 pounds) in weight, homeless and feeling disconnected from the entire world. I felt alone and the adults who could have helped my situation only had opinions about my situation. Today, I am more than blessed to be extraordinarily successful. All of my success came from understanding one principal, we are all connected.

Dear Reader, as I was sleeping in the public trashcan on a dark road in small town Texas, I began to wonder if I was equally as smart as all the other people who were not living in trashcans. And then it dawned on me that I could do exactly what they did. In fact, I ended up doing much better than they might have done because they could not go through what I am going through right now.

There is no separation. This has been physically proven by science. It is called Entanglement. I think the reason that we don't realize how connected we all are because we are so distracted by the human level of our own experiences. I have taken it upon myself to be the person to clear up this confusion. There is no separation, dear reader. There is just you and I — and we are one. The fact that we are already light and we are already complete is so powerful to me that I travel the entire world making sure people understand this fact.

I would like to take credit for stopping a major war or two, and who knows, maybe I have. However, I can say this. I have been successful in letting people know that all of us are energy and what we do to one another, we are also doing unto ourselves. When you hurt, I hurt. When I hurt you intentionally, I forfeit one of my own dreams. Anything that I can see in you, I also see it in me, even if I do not want to admit this fact. The mere fact that I can see it in you is also scientific proof that it is in my awareness so that I may be able to see it in you. Human beings can only see the things that are in their consciousness. We see each other's flaws because we can always see we have that same flaw. Now, I have a message for you.

We are not human beings that have consciousness; we are a consciousness that have human bodies. I want you to know this from the bottom of my heart. Our human experiences are just that— a way for us to experience being semi-separated from the great creative source, in order to experience how beautiful the creative source is.

When one is to think of the ocean, one will also think of the waves. While you are thinking, you will naturally think that the wave is separate from the ocean. Yet, the wave *is* the ocean. You can never separate yourself from the creative source, no more than I can separate water from a soft drink.

When I teach around the world, I teach people to let go of individual survival and to respect the suffering of others as their own suffering. Currently, the world is receiving its collective consciousness. We let 40,000 children a day die from starvation, because as a collective, we have decided that children dying from starvation is normal.

Here is my final message to you. You are as good as the other person. You are perfect and already made whole. You have been taught the opposite but with an open mind; you can help me change the world.

The ironic thing is that everyone is looking for God, but everyone already has God in his heart and consciousness. How much better can you and I make this world if we both accept that what is in God is in us? How much better can this world be if we fully accept that you and I have always been conscious and you and I always will be? How much differently would we treat one another if we realized that we are all connected?

Walk this path with me. Help me change the world by helping me tell everyone in the world that they were are all complete. We are not separate from the world. We are one. This is how I am making a difference in the world. Regardless of the country I find myself in that is the one thing that always remains the same. We are all

3

connected. I feel it. I know it and there is nothing that anyone can ever do to change my mind about that. I would much rather be wrong about treating people like they are ourselves, than to be right and continue to leave the world separated world it has become like it already is.

You can plant better. You can dominate.

Antonio T Smith Jr
www.fb.com/theatsjr

IGNITION 2

Your Mind Is Your Most Precious Commodity

Betty Riddick

My name is Betty Riddick an entrepreneur, speaker, coach, and author. Through my story I would like to offer you hope in an otherwise dark world. At the outset, I want to instill in you that you can be delivered from stress, depression and anxiety if you will just believe in yourself and the Almighty God.

I am a living example of someone who survived all these things when I placed my trust in the Almighty and in myself thereafter. The greatest thing about that is that I get to share it with everyone who is in a similar or worse situation and help them to help themselves. I do it through speaking to people and I'm thankful that I get to bring positive energy to my audiences.

Let me continue to share a little more of my story with you by taking you back some 25 years ago in my life when I was so depressed that I literally lost my mind and had to be admitted to a mental hospital 4 times. This happened three times in Virginia and once in Pennsylvania.

I couldn't cope with life situations. I was a single mom, working hard as the breadwinner. I was continuously stressed out and in relationships that were not good for me. I could not say no to anyone and ended up stretching myself to limits beyond anything I could manage. This drove me to a dark place in my heart and mind and I felt hopeless and helpless and eventually I gave into the darkness and resolved to stay there just because I didn't have the energy to do anything else.

The doctors treating me at the time compared my life to that of a pressure cooker and likened what happened to me to that of an explosive one. The diagnosis in medical terms was bipolar disorder and I was told that I would be on medication for the rest of my life.

I refused the medication and the psychiatry treatment and did the one thing most of don't do when we are faced with similar or worse situations. I turned to prayer and God and I am happy to say that that is what delivered me from the ordeal that I found myself in. I know that that maybe hard to believe but that is certainly the truth about my life and I have no qualms about how it turned out for me or sharing it with you because I have three important affirmations that I use in my life and that I want to share with you before I end this story.

The first is that you should always live in the consciousness of your Creator. His presence in your life and matters of your life are important and are a guiding source for you in all matters. God always shows you the right way so you should be conscious of Him.

The second is that when you are stressed you need to remember that you are equally blessed. If you really took the time to count your blessings you would see that you have a lot more to be thankful for than you have to be worried or stressed about.

The last is that you should accept whatever decisions your Creator makes for you without disappointment. The truth is He does know what's best for you and will never set you on a path that is destructive for you.

I currently work for myself in a business that helps others who have walked in my path. Always remember that life's obstacles are character building and that when you apply the basic things in your life, you will find that your mind is the most precious commodity that you have. Stay stress free!

Betty Riddick
www.bettyriddick.com
riddickbjr@gmail.com
001(404) 839-9739

IGNITION 3

The Fight Of A Lifetime

Brandi Rae Blouch

One of life's biggest blessings is being able to bring hope to people through empowering information and healing. This is my purpose and gift and this is my story.

I was diagnosed with a bipolar disorder when I was 30 years old. They were just words to me at the time and I had no idea what impact it would really have on my life until I began the prescribed treatment. At first, I tried to live as normally as possible and then as I began a series of treatments, I found that normal was not possible anymore. Lost relationships, a broken spirit and an empty inner self were just the smaller side effects of the treatment. I felt out of control but I also nurtured the will to survive, the hope that there had to be an easier way to survive the storm. I shuffled between doctors and treatments for 10 years before I reached "managed stability." Nobody can imagine the other changes that would rapidly invade my being and body.

I gained 50 pounds rapidly and it didn't help that I was suffering from severe chronic constipation as well. Sometimes the pain is both excruciating and unbearable. Treatment for it is undoubtedly humiliating and solutions are quite temporary and not at all healing.

I additionally, suffered bouts of high blood pressure. Both my psychiatrist and physician were in denial, each blaming the other for the medication being prescribed to treat me. I was rapidly reaching a tethers end. I needed to find my own solutions to this horrible ordeal and though I knew I had the answers within, I struggled to reach inside of me and take the action needed.

I played fate right into my own hands when I began nutritional research. Stumbling upon the Institute of Integrative Nutrition was a game changer. For one year, I empowered myself with information and tried over a hundred theories and things finally began to work in my favor. The blood pressure finally stabilized and I began to drop off the pounds. What was the difference?

The shocking but simple difference is that I changed the way I looked at medicine and food. I reversed their roles in my life. Whereas medicine was my hope to being healed, I realized that it was actually food that was my hope to being healed. It's quite simple but the most powerful truth that there is. To top it all, I became a health coach and resolved to help others to begin their own journeys of recovery, too.

I stepped out of the shadows and definitely out of my own way and shared my story in a book. I didn't care if I bared my soul. All I wanted was to help people realize that they too could help themselves without needing to escalate the condition and without sacrificing their dignity.

I had to demystify all the misconceptions around mental illnesses. I had to remind people that they could be productive, and that they could have a healthy life even with a bipolar disorder. I realized that so many just needed to feel understood because the condition leaves so much in its wake in the form of broken relationships, families and lives.

Mental illness does not discriminate. It doesn't care if you're poor or rich or what part of the world you're from or whether you're a celebrity or a peasant. Bipolar disorder has a very strong genetic component. But that isn't the tell-all. The genetic predisposition makes you more susceptible for the illness. The environmental factors are what becomes the trigger for this illness.

Today, I provide information about bipolar disorder, what it is, the symptoms, how it can be treated and the truth about medication. I also teach people how to take care of themselves whilst on medication. This is not an illness that goes away. It is a lifelong condition that requires consistent care and everyone has a right to that.

We are now looking at people holistically. We are not just focusing on an illness that requires medication.

When I set out on a life of service, to help others get their power back, I am not sure if I ever really knew if I would really make a difference. People come and go in our lives and that's true for those of us who are healers and helpers. I do my best to be open and honest and allow myself to be vulnerable and willing to share my own trauma and experiences. It is most important for people to know they don't have to suffer in silence. They are not defective in any way and this is not a punishment.

The most important thing I want to share is that hope and attitude are the most important things you can exercise when you are faced with challenges. Empower yourself with what you need to know to help yourself and most of all reach within yourself for your strength and do what you know is right for you.

Brandi Rae Blouch.
www.nourishyoursweetspot.com
email: nourishyoursweetspot@hotmail.com

IGNITION 4

If It Was To Be, It Was Up To Me

Cami Baker

Imagine if you will, an adorable little two-year old blonde girl. Big brown eyes. All full of love and excited to see her Mommy picking her up from daycare. I was the Mommy. As I scooped her up in my arms to take her for our normal fun evening at home, I held her in front of me. Face to face, you know, when you are so close you can smell each other? And what I smelled was the alcohol on my own breath.

I knew she didn't know what the smell was. Not yet. But she would, and she would be embarrassed. She wouldn't be taken care of as she deserved, possibly abused or surely neglected. In that moment, I knew something had to change. I had to change. I had to fix myself. If it was to be, it was up to me!

Putting the bottle down, and putting my big girl panties on was undoubtably the hardest thing I have ever done. It was the most rewarding, life changing and life shifting venture, not just for me, not just for my daughter, but also for the millions that I have come to serve.

Alcoholics are some of the hardest working, creative and loving people on the planet. We make up about 10% of the population that literally have an allergy to alcohol. Just like someone who breaks out from nuts or shellfish, we break out in handcuffs and just simply must learn why that happens and how to not have it happen anymore. The problem is that when we are actively drinking, all that hard work and creativity is put into getting our fix, hiding it and living a life of pure misery. The love that we have is so deep and strong, that that is sometimes why we drink. We just don't know how to handle our feelings and emotions and it is easier to numb and run.

With that said, when the lucky alcoholic is given the gift of life by having the obsession overcome, there isn't a single reason you can't move from saying "Good God it's morning!" to "Good morning God!"

When I sobered up, I got a JOB in a real estate office. I was just about unemployable when I got sober. I only had a job because my boss was my boyfriend and drinking buddy. Now sober, I was given the gift of being around people who simply didn't drink. They weren't lying about not drinking, hiding it, talking about it, encouraging it. They just simply lived without it and that was a new concept for me, yet one that I found supportive and encouraging.

I started reading books again for the first time since high school (I was now 32). I had a cassette of "Feel the fear and do it anyway!" by Susan Jefferies that I listened to literally hundreds of times. My boss gave me a simple pamphlet that I was able to read in a couple hours call "You2 Squared" by Price Pritchett that I have now given to people over the years. I listened to Tony Robbins and a couple years into sobriety I even walked on fire with a Tony Robbins group.

I learned that when you want something, you find someone who already has that which you want and you follow their lead. Whether it is reading a book, listening, watching videos, going to seminars or noticing the people in your everyday life, it is a matter of hanging out with those that you aspire to emulate.

Over the last 17 years I have been a real estate agent in the top 5% every year. I built a network marketing team of 10,000 worldwide and personally recruited 131 people. I have stepped into my true purpose of being a wisdom carrier, coach, mentor, and strategist. I've spoken on hundreds of stages, worked with thousands of people world-wide and I have been on HGTV's House Hunters, Celebrity Apprentice as a guest judge, in Success From Home magazine, written the book "Mingle to Millions. I'm now also a guest host on the Happiness Jungle TV Show with one of the best friends I've ever had. I share these things not to impress you, but to impress upon you that if I can do it, anyone can.

It has not all be easy or a steady rise to the top. I wish I could say I have 17 years of continuous sobriety but I don't. It would be nice to have been responsible with every decision, every dollar and every relationship but I have had weak moments. But this is what I know for sure, and that is that the more I know, the more I know I don't know and the more I know I need to know! Good judgement comes from experience and experience comes from poor judgement. If you're not failing, SHAME ON YOU! It means you are playing it safe. You are not trying. You are not growing. Successful people are simply people who have tried and failed a LOT, learned from the trying and got up from the times it didn't work.

Every time I get interviewed, they always ask, "What is the one piece of advice you would give our viewers, listeners or readers?" My answer is always the same, "Change your playgrounds and playmates". Meaning, who are you hanging out with will determine who you are. If you hang out with 5 negative broke people, you will be the 6th. When you hang out with people who are planning their year, goal setting, listening to motivational music, people and books or just simply laughing, enjoying the sun and being lifted by the sound of a child's laughter then that is who you become too.

If it was to be, it was up to me. If it is to be for you, it is up to you. We can make excuses, or we can make it happen. We can ask "what's wrong with me?", or we can ask "how can I grow, expand and become more?". Our brain answers the questions we ask it. Instead of "Why am I so stupid, lazy, fat or broke, ask how you can become better. Strive for F3, become fearless, fabulous and on fire.

Cami Baker
facebook.com/cami.baker.56
cami@camibaker.com
1-603-785-2598

IGNITION 5

The Birth Of A Health Muse

Cheryl Meyer

Six years ago, I was a workaholic. I loved what I did for a living, made friends with other workaholics, and they supported and sustained me through the years. I argued that stress moved me forward to greater results, and I wasn't paying attention to the costs I would pay down the line.

Working 24/7 came with a price-I was eating junk food, the chemicals took their toll, and I added unnecessary and unwanted pounds. I was eating at hyper-speed in exactly the same way I was working all day to get all my tasks accomplished. To top it all, I didn't exercise.

Because I wasn't paying attention to my body, I missed all the signs that inflammation was setting in. First, I had a reaction to all under arm deodorants. Then it was my mascara. Later, I couldn't be around people wearing fragrance because I couldn't breathe. I woke up one morning and my tongue and lips were swollen, and it turned out that I was now reacting to the fabric softener. Soon, every bone and every muscle in my body hurt. It felt like I had been

16

beaten up with a baseball hat. I had diabetes. I had high blood pressure. I was overweight. I just felt worse by the day. It was now that it dawned on me that I was in trouble and needed help.

It didn't help that my doctor thought it was all in my head. She prescribed pills, including steroids and I just refused to take them. I just had a feeling that I needed to take matters into my own hands and take responsibility for getting well by myself. So, I turned my jewelry business over to my staff and started researching. I didn't even have a clue what I was looking for. I just knew that I wasn't going to live a life of pain and pills.

I found the Functional Medicine community and listened to 20 different symposiums. I figured out I probably had autoimmune disease and 'leaky gut" kept coming up in the lectures. What was leaky gut, I asked and if I had it, what could I do about it? I learned that two things that I could control were stress, and toxins. So I dug in. I was appalled to find hundreds of toxins in my life, and set out to eliminate and replace them one by one.

Today, 6 years later, I am a health in progress, married to a fabulous man, winding down my jewelry business and passionate about everything I have learned along the way. I am living a life of balance. I have lost 45 pounds without dieting. I no longer hurt.

I have a fabulous functional MD and she is getting to the root cause of my ailments. Our relationship is a partnership. I want to help people make simple lifestyle changes to dramatically improve the quality of their lives.

I am coaching others to be responsible for their own health and their own life. I work with them to have the same benefits of healthier living that I have found for myself.

17

I read like a fiend. In lieu of retiring I decided to help others make lifestyle changes that would improve the quality of their lives. At 67, I went back to school to become a Certified Health Coach through IIN, The Institute for Integrative Nutrition®. I have tried dozens of different things on my own journey to a healthier, happier life. I have researched all of the triggers of inflammation and autoimmune disease and I have written an award-winning book that is published on Amazon, *It Feels Good to Feel Good: Learn to Eliminate Toxins, Reduce Inflammation, and Feel Great Again*. I offer a free workbook to anyone that buys my book so that it is not daunting to eliminate the toxins one by one. It's all about toxic load, so every toxin eliminated is one step closer to health.

I have found my purpose. I graduated in 2017. In the last year, I have done 40 podcasts talking about toxins, and participated in 8 summits to spread my information. I have spoken locally at hospitals, at "lunch and learns" for businesses, and at churches. I work one on one with private clients. I am now writing my second book about how I live a toxin free life. People all over are responding positively to my message and that makes me so happy.

My journey has given me three key things that I would like to share with everyone.

- Own your own health, and don't let anyone tell you that you can't get well. Where ever you are in your health, it is not how the story has to end.
- Learn to listen to your body. It has tremendous wisdom. If you feed it the right nutrients, it wants to heal. Garbage in, garbage out.
- Clean up the toxins in your life. Eat organic, and eliminate the other toxins that are everywhere. It's all about toxic load. Eliminate them one at a time. Your body will note the

difference fairly quickly. You don't need to live a life of pain and pills. There is a better way.

Cheryl Meyer
www.cherylmhealthmuse.com
facebook@Cherylmhealthmuse

IGNITION 6

The Power to Effect Change Using Your Talents

Chinyere Helyn Njoku

The one purpose we all have in common is service. I am sure you will agree that this is the reason why each of us was born with talents. Surprisingly, many people are not aware of what their talents are. Some who know what their talents are, are not using them. However, there exists a group of people, who know what their talents are, and are using them to empower others. They have discovered the power that lies in the use of their talents. It is, therefore, imperative that we learn to discover, develop, and deploy our talents for good, as doing so will enable us to live a life of purpose.

Myles Monroe, of blessed memory, once said that the richest place on earth is the graveyard. Wow!!! Imagine the many books, businesses, songs, and products that will be buried in the grave, simply because some people were reluctant to use their talents.

Here is my Talentpreneurial experience of how I discovered one of my talents and how I put it to work. It is my hope that you will be inspired to discover, develop, and deploy your talents in such a way that you can make positive changes in the lives of many people.

I held a managerial position in a US Bank, where I worked a 9-5 job, for a little over five years. During the fourth year, I found myself thinking that there is surely more to life than just having to wake up early every morning, go to work for 9-12 hours, return home exhausted, barely have enough sleep, and then, repeat that whole cycle all over again. Pointless! Wouldn't you say? I also imagined how I could harness all the talents, skills, experiences, and the lessons I had gathered over the years, to make a difference in people's lives. I began to have meditative sessions, where I thought about those activities I love to engage in, and how I could turn them into a service or product.

When you find yourself on this path of self-discovery, I want you to remember that you will be confronted with many obstacles and objections. However, the biggest obstacle you will have to overcome is YOURSELF. Here is why. As you meditate and think about your areas of strength and how you can put them to work, you will discover that fear and self-doubt will creep in. You will, instinctively, come up with so many reasons why you should not, start that business, develop that product, write that song, coach people, and so on. Most importantly, you will find yourself asking questions about how you will finance your vision and how you will sustain yourself whilst you try to make things work. You will also be concerned about whether you will generate a viable income and whether or not you will be successful. When this happens, always remember that it takes courage to succeed. Get a grip of yourself and shake off such discouraging thoughts by believing that you are the solution to the cries of many, you have got what it takes to help people, you are enough, and you can do it.

One faithful Sunday afternoon, I had an epiphany to publish a goodwill message on video, advising people to use their talents positively. To my surprise, after posting the 13-minute video on Facebook, it received so many views and comments. I received requests to produce more inspiring videos and that is exactly what I did. Those requests made me realize that there is power in the use of my communicative talents to inspire people to act. With that, I went ahead and registered my business, Helyn's Corner, LLC. I did not stop there, as I kept thinking of ways I could do more.

It was rough and tough. I made many sacrifices, which included resigning from my job, living on a shoe-string budget for about nine months, going hungry with no food to eat on many occasions, forgoing my sleep, and not going shopping for new clothing. There were many nights I cried myself to sleep. Nevertheless, I remained resolute and continued to channel my meager resources into creating my book and online academy, the Talentpreneurship Academy.

Against all odds, I completed my book and launched it, both virtually and physically. I made over $10,000 in income. In addition, requests were extended to me to be a part of two book writing collaborations, three online/TV interviews, speaking engagements, and co-hosting on a radio show. Human beings do not have the ability to be omnipresent. However, I was able to ignite the power in my talents and make my materials ubiquitous. It gladdens my heart to know that by using my talents, I have been able to inspire people to start businesses, begin relationships, and create their online shows. You can do the same. Remember, great things happen when you use your talents and walk in your purpose.

Decide today that you will start to use your talents for good. You will be amazed how circumstances and people will begin to align with your intentions. When I decided to write my book, I began to carry out research, and was introduced to a Coach, who coached me in writing my book. Now, I coach people who want to write their books. If you refuse to focus on the areas in which you lack, you can achieve whatever you set your mind to.

There are four reasons why you should use your talents:

- You become a solution provider
- You are relevant
- You make a difference in people's lives
- You live a purpose driven life.

In closing, here is a quote by Winston Churchill – *"Success is not final, failure is not fatal. It is the courage to continue that counts."* That's my story, and I am sticking to it!

Chinyere Helyn Njoku (Lady Helyn of Helyn's Corner)
www.helynscorner.com
www.talentpreneurship-academy.thinkific.com
Facebook: https://www.facebook.com/helynscorner
YouTube: Chinyere Njoku / Helyn's Corner
Instagram: @ladyhelyn

IGNITION 7

Born To Defy All The Odds

Dr. Farookh Sensei

I was born to defy all the odds because all through my life I have done whatever others have said or felt I could not. By the Grace of the Almighty God, whenever I have defied the odds and continue to do so, I have been successful and I believe I always will be.

Growing up, we were always moving from one state to another while dad was pursuing his career with Indian Air Force. Once dad joined a company in Kuwait, my brother and I tested freedom and began bunking school. We were eventually caught, expelled and finally went to work in our uncle's business. I wanted to pursue my studies so I attended interview with few well-established schools but failed in all of them. The only school that opened its door was a public school where Malayalam was the medium of instruction. I couldn't read or write Malayalam but I had no option other than joining this school. I managed the first two years, but when it came to the public exam, I failed. I tried again and again, and at last made it to the borderline.

While I was in the 10th Grade, I found my passion in Karate and joined the very first club in my hometown. Bruce Lee was my inspiration. Without support or money from my family, I eventually sold the only gift my dad gave me to pay my registration fee at the karate school. It was one of the best decisions I ever made because it became the cornerstone of my life. I didn't have money to pay my monthly tuition fees so I painted posters, banners and advertising boards for the club instead.

After 4 months of regular training, I entered my very first belt test and failed. I persevered for another 4 months and when our grand master Shihan Bonnie Roberts, 8th Dan Black Belt came to India for the exam, I didn't have money to pay for it. As luck would have it, my cousin gifted me 50 rupees and you can guess what I used that for.

In grade 11 at age 16, I turned entrepreneur and opened my own karate club. This was my first experience at teaching others who were elder to me. My instructor didn't quite like the idea that I had opened a club of my own. He also ridiculed my dream to become a karate champion. He said it would never happen. In order to pursue my martial art career, I got out of his way and joined a club run by his master. Nothing was going to stop me from my dreams. I was determined. Inside of me, I knew I was born for success.

I was right because in 1987 I went on to become the heavyweight national karate champion of India. In 1991 I won Gold Medal in the All India Kobudo (Weapon) Championship and in 1992 & 1993 I won 2nd place in the national level championships. I was not only defying all odds, I was fast establishing clubs of my own and becoming a force to reckon with. After 4 decades of karate in my life, I broke record after record, winning international recognition on so many levels.

Karate was just one passion in which I was excelling. For a real career, I was building dreams of becoming a pilot and when I took the exam and passed I was so sure that I would be selected in the interview. As soon as the examiners saw me and learned my height, I was disqualified for being too tall to sit in a cockpit. I also had just 10% vision in my right eye and this was a spoke in the wings so to speak. I was broken but not defeated.

Working for an airline has always been my dream. When Dad, returned to India from Kuwait and introduced me to IATA (International Air Transport Association) courses, I saw a second chance to enter into the airline industry. There were no IATA schools in my hometown so I opted for self-studies. I wasn't successful in the first round of the exam and of course, failed again. Undeterred, I reappeared for the course. This time, I decided to master the subject by teaching the same course to some of my close friends. The more I taught, the more I learned. Teaching airline subjects became my new passion.

Teaching helped me and my students to pass the IATA exam and finally achieve the diploma I needed to enter into the airline industry.

My doors into aviation opened up when SATM (School of Airline and Travel Management), partnered with Air India and organized a 10-day training program in Cochin (India). I was the only candidate to score a 100%. SATM offered me the position of chief instructor and regional manager. I had finally landed my first real job.

With four years of hard-work, I became the only person in the world to earn 14 IATA qualifications. LIMCA Book of Records recognized this achievement as a world record. I went on to break my own record 7 times. Today I have a total of 41 IATA Certifications. This record is yet to be broken by anyone.

In 1988, I joined the London School of Management in the UK as chief instructor of aviation studies. The world outside India finally opened up to me. In 2002 the world of the Middle East called on me and I joined Qatar Airways, conducting training in 50 odd countries around the world. I count those years amongst the most accomplished and most exciting times of my career because all my experience there finally led me to where I am now.

At age 50, I opted for early retirement and am a full-time entrepreneur, another dream, and goal I had established along the way. The difference is that now I am working towards leaving a legacy that I pray will matter to the world even when I am no more. Today I am a results and leadership coach, certified by John Maxwell and Les Brown and I trade under the name Ledge International. I help clients to achieve their goals much faster and easier than they ever think is possible. I am also the founder of my own online chat show called Ignition. On this show, I interview authors, speakers, and entrepreneurs about their experiences and give my viewers the opportunity to motivate and inspire themselves to go after their own dreams over and over again. Along the way, I have documented my experiences and anecdotes into 4 books that are full of knowledge, skills, and aptitude that I openly believe will help those that read it. These books are readily available on Amazon and I invite everyone to take advantage of them.

Finally, I leave you with one of my Quotes "Your will and skill will take you to the top, only your passion and purpose will keep at the top". My purpose in life is to help others find their calling. What's yours?

Dr. Farookh Sensei
www.farookhsensei.com
team@farookhsensei.com

IGNITION 8

How I DISRUPPT Lives For The Better

Harish Mehta

I have never been just a PERFORMER. I have always been an ACHIEVER and as I ring in the 60th year of my LIFE, I realize with joy that it has been quite a journey and that I have much to share with you. And no, this is not in any way one of those life time achievement stories, in which I prepare to say my piece and then throw in the towel. I have much to offer still and this portion of my STORY is just a pause to happily reflect.

I was born in Delhi, India and graduated with HONS in Commerce in 1978. An all-round performer, I was a keen league cricketer at school and university level. The serious business of having a career started soon after University as I joined the banking world in Kolkata. I worked at 2 banks and each time I moved I was progressing within the sector. Within 3 years became the branch manager at a prominent bank in MUMBAI and worked there for almost 20 years before I quit the sector completely, and moved on.

I joined some of my friends in business and together we built and grew a **children's** LIFESTYLE clothing business. When we started

29

we were doing a modest turnover of about Rs 8 million by the end of my tenure, almost 10 years later, we were happily turning at Rs 2500million. The brand today is still a force to reckon with and although I am not with them anymore, it is still a matter of joy and pride for me to have been a part of that venture. It taught me many lessons and prepared me for the kind of role I would play today in helping others to grow their **businesses**.

I did some extensive travelling after retiring from the children's clothing business and learnt a more about **leadership** as I met people from all walks of life. Interacting with people internationally opened up my mind to a whole new world of possibilities and I started to realize that I could use what I had done to help others become successful at business. So, when I returned to India I began engaging with people I thought could use my help and this spurred me on and inspired me to work on myself also. My purpose was to help people ascertain where they were and where they wanted to go.

I had to do a lot of learning myself in order to help other businesses progress effectively. I found my first coach, Brad Sugars at ActionCOACH and learnt the process and art of business coaching from him. The thirst to learn more and be more took over and so I went on training with some of the finest coaches in world-**Marshall Goldsmith Bob Proctor, Robin Sharma, Michael Losier, John C Maxwell and Les Brown** are just a few. It was **Les Brown** who pointed out that I had a strong voice with which I could **influence** thousands of people and I became a **motivational coach and speaker**. I have never looked back since then nor doubted any of the things I am doing with my life today. I am confident that I am exactly where I am supposed to be and that I am doing exactly what I was meant to do. I have made a place of value for myself and I am happy that through it, I can also add value wherever I go. It's been one glorious gift after the next.

My personal favorite in the journey though, is working with the youth at personal mastery. I enjoy the challenge of engaging with minds that work so differently from my generation of leaders and am always pleasantly surprised at their insights. I have always felt that because the future of the world depends on them, we need to fuel their passions, help them give it life and shape and be there to support them as they soar into unchartered territories tomorrow.

I firmly believe in the application of 6 mental faculties to achieve anything you set out to do in your life. **IMAGINATION, INTUITION, WILL, MEMORY, REASON AND PERCEPTION, when used effectively**, will help you reap the results you want with your goals. I also inculcate that everything is energy. If you remember that your thoughts begin with it, your emotions amplify it and your actions increase its momentum, then you will understand the power of using your thoughts effectively.

Whilst my program **DiSRUPPt** is centered around the above thoughts, it is also a series of powerful formulae, which when applied, help people to make breakthroughs in their lives and careers. I often get asked why I apply this formula to my training and the answer is very simple. Nothing is achieved without proper action and what I want to do is **DiSRUPPt** behaviors, like **procrastination, gossiping, worrying, criticizing, fear, self-doubt and replace them with positive ones like happiness, self-belief, confidence, fearlessness, drive, courage, clarity and commitment**. This is based on the simple premise that what I am DiSRUPPt ing will bring positive change and momentum for the greater good of those DiSRUPPt ed.

When I wake up every day, I renew my Commitment to creating a new U through me. I have made this choice willingly and it makes me happy to think that somewhere in the future someone will carry

31

my legacy forward and DiSRUPPt the lives of others, too. In the end, we are all working for the greater good of the world and I often think it would be great when all of us in the world WILL do MORE every day to help that along.

Harish Mehta
www.harishmehta.com
harish@harishmehta.com
+919920917477

IGNITION 9

Out Of Nothing Into Something

Henry Agassi

I was born in a small village in Africa to teenage parents, and I was born in an environment with a great deal of poverty and hopelessness. When I observed my grandfather, he gave me a sense of hope and taught me to that be in difficult situations does not have to define me. He taught me to focus on my dreams. I remember that we would often travel to the city at different times of the year, especially Christmas time to buy clothes and food stuff and I would see all the beautiful things in the city. I noticed that the city kids dressed in beautiful school uniforms. I desired those things too and I wanted to be like those kids, so much so that when I went back to the village my mind would be in the city.

But we didn't have a house in the city, so my grandfather rented a one bedroom for us in a four-bedroom house. This house was rundown, the door was off so the house was wide open. Six of us shared one bedroom and one towel, and when you are sharing one towel with six people, it gets wet before it gets to you. I would sometimes run out into the sun to dry off because I didn't want to use the wet towel. This house had no running water, no electricity and no indoor plumbing. Water was scarce, I remember sometimes we would have a small bowl of water and we had to share that water between six people. That meant that we would only wash the parts of our bodies that were exposed; our legs, hands and faces and then we'd rub Vaseline and make ourselves shine. We called that rub and shine.

We soon returned to the village because my grandfather had no money to send me to another school in the city after graduation. I returned to a school that had no doors, no windows, no indoor plumbing. I got sent home many times because I couldn't pay my tuition which was equivalent to five dollars.

I was in that school for 3 years before my father whom I hadn't seen for close to ten years because he was living in Toronto, came home. He came to Nigeria and once he saw how I lived, arranged for me to go to school in the city again. I was overjoyed because it meant having three meals a day, having my own bed and of course, my own towel. That was a big deal for me. However, I suspected that I would struggle to cope at school and I was right. I felt inferior because of where I came from and that soon crept into my school performance. I saw myself as a loser and a failure and sure enough my results reflected that. It killed my self-esteem and I had no idea if I would ever graduate. Maths and English were my weaknesses and at that time you had to pass both those subjects to get to the next level.

I was however determined and I took charge of myself. I didn't want to go back to village you see so I began learning 5 words from the dictionary every day. My English did improve and when my teachers saw the effort I was making, they too assisted me. My principal had an especially positive effect on me with powerful words. She would tell us to watch our thoughts thoughts for they became our words, our words became our actions, our actions for they became our characters and our characters for they became our destinies. She'd also tell us never to be ordinary, to always try to be extraordinary, and she'd go on and say how the difference between being ordinary and extraordinary is that extraordinary meant that you would get ahead in life with just a little more effort.

Those words stuck with me. I started striving to be extraordinary, and she told me how important it is to monitor my thoughts because they'll ultimately become my destiny. And that's true because we don't get in life what we want, we get in life what we are.

Today I have a BA from the University of Windsor. I have partnered with and have been mentored by some of the best people in the world, including Mr. Les Brown. To me, he is one of the best speakers on the planet and he inspired me to travel around the world inspiring people to pursue their own dreams. My desire is to do for others what my grandfather did for me by motivating and inspiring others to change their voices and therefore their lives.

Here are some of the things that helped me get to where I am today.
- **Focus**-I was focused by creating a mental GPS of where I wanted to be in life.
- **Faith**- I accepted myself but refused to refuse to accept the situation in which I was born into as my destiny and believed that things would get better for me if I didn't give up. And I had faith in God through constant prayers.
- **Action**- I took action to improve my situation. I worked hard in school to acquire education because I realized that education is the key that would unlock many doors for me.

Henry Agassi
www.henryagassi.com
henry@henryagassi.com

IGNITION 10

Be Exactly Who You Were Meant To Be

Dr. Ira Roach III

"If you are who everyone wants you to be, who will be you?" This was the question posed to me by my coach in 2016. It's an invaluable question and I think everybody should ask themselves this every now and then to ensure that they are on track with who they would like to be. You see, the more you seek to be others, the more you miss out on who you are and what you have to offer the world.

In 2015 after years of searching for ways of becoming the best version of myself, I came across Daniel Ally's story and was inspired enough to drop him an email. I was pleasantly surprised to receive a call from him and this call was quite an eye opener. He asked me if I wanted to become a millionaire and told me I had to change my mind-set to change my reality. This was his condition for coaching me. I enrolled on his six-month program but didn't follow through with the requirements properly. Needless to say, success wasn't happening at that point in time.

Statistics show that 98% of people don't achieve their goals, only 6% achieve their childhood dreams and 53% of young Americans give up on their dreams completely. It seemed I would fast be a statistic if I didn't do anything about that fast.

My problem wasn't that I didn't want to rich. My problem was that I had resigned myself to an impoverished lifestyle and mindset which I was convinced was my lot in life. Work at the ministry was tiring and I was failing at the entrepreneurial efforts I was making within the ministry as well. I moved back home to live it "small" and to refocus and re-strategize. I was tired of living this way and I wanted time to come up with a new plan.

I enrolled in the local SBA ambassador program which allowed me to enlist with a mentor and she was awesome! I met with her once a week and each week I had homework to turn in. This lady assisted me in re-branding my name and obtaining liability insurance. I absolutely loved going to talk to her and it was encouraging and enlightening. I implemented the tools that she gave me and planned an event for Saturday, September 16, 201. I paid $150.00 for the venue and no one showed up. I was devastated because I had done everything I was supposed to do including advertising the event properly and still no one attended.

I had to LEVEL up and so I joined the Les Brown Unlimited Team. I enrolled into the Les Brown Unlimited Team because I wanted to surround myself with a tribe that believed in me, that would hold me accountable for the action steps in becoming the best version of myself and that would support and teach me how to tell my story. The Les Brown Team did this. I remember signing on, going through the orientation and then taking my first course which was Speak Your Way to Unlimited Wealth. I was and still am in awe of Les Brown and I knew immediately I was on the right track. I could feel that I was near breakthrough.

I completed this first course in two days. My new tribe on Facebook was congratulating me and I was overwhelmed with the kind of support I was receiving. I finally felt a sense of belonging and honestly sometimes that's all someone needs to make their breakthrough.

I attended the Les Brown Certification event in April of 2018 and I discovered my "Power Voice" during that weekend.

My family did not know how important attending this event was to me, but my close friends and colleagues were excited. I arrived at the certification met my SBL group members who were in attendance and celebrated with my new tribe. I took the tools that I received that weekend and this time I have implemented them.

I have learned that I am bigger than titles and anyone's opinion. Since being a part of this tribe, I have joined a web series recently I was nominated for a best actor award. I came home after the certification and signed on three clients. I have a definite date for an exit strategy from my current job and I have enrolled with a branding and marketing coach to help me establish my name and business.

My latest book project may or may not be in publication when this is released but it's entitled, "Daddy Knows Best: *What Every Boy Needs from his Dad.*" This book project is about helping absent fathers to understand that they too are bigger than labels and it's not too late to live their dreams.

I want to share a Les Brown quote to end my chapter here because I think many readers will resonate with it in the same way that I did. "Don't let the opinions of others become your reality." I had many titles in my past but I want the world to understand that sometimes those titles mean nothing if you can't get past them and live your dreams and goals. I also want everyone to understand the power that coaching has to transform people and to help them find their purpose. I encourage everyone to find their coach and to live their dreams.

Dr. Ira Roach III
www.driraroachiii.com
ira.inspires@gmail.com
+1-302-217-8990

IGNITION 11

A Vision For More

Jayson Gerald

If you're like me, and it's likely that you are because I am nothing out of the ordinary, you grew up being told by family members or teachers that you can be anything you want to be, if you just put your mind to it. If you are anything like me, which you very well may have been, you probably told yourself that that was a fairytale or that it was a bunch of nonsense.

See, when I was growing up I always thought that in order to be rich or successful you had to grow up in a family that was already rich or powerful. I thought the best I could hope for was a mediocre 9-5 job that paid the bills and allowed me to have a family and be happy. I believed that myth for nearly 37 years. 10 years of my life were spent battling depression, drug and alcohol abuse, monetary poverty and relationship woes. I realized midway through life that the fairytale would have been absolutely true had I really put my mind to it. All you have to do is just do it!

I believe most people are programmed from a very early age to believe that there are limits in life, that the best way to do things is always the safe way. Never take too big of a risk. Never put yourself in a position where the potential for failure exists. I took this approach for almost 30 years.

I lived a fairly mediocre life, even though it was peppered with some self-defeating decisions I had made along the way that made my life incredibly difficult. But after much struggle, I finally had the basics – a family, a home, a steady job and a lot of untapped, idle potential. This is where most people stop in life. This is their pinnacle, this is their summit. This is where most people stop trying to achieve things in life and play everything super-safe so that they can enjoy staying where they are until the end of their days. That is OK but I was from the 1% of the population that felt I needed to do more, achieve more and go after my vision for more.

One of the most valuable lessons I've learned in life is that you're not truly living your life unless you are *actively pursuing* your dreams, visions and goals. Unless you are actively participating in shaping your future in a way that creates a feeling of fulfillment and happiness, you're wasting your life. You are all but dead on the inside, your spirit is lifeless. You get up every morning and go through the routine of drinking coffee, getting ready for work, working for a company that can easily replace you within a couple days or weeks no matter how long you have been with them, and then you come home after 8 or 9 hours, eat dinner with your family and then stare into the magic screen on the wall or in the palm of your hand until you fall asleep. Then, the next morning, you repeat that. Over and over and over again until you *physically* die. Sound familiar?

If this is you, and you make the conscious decision that you don't want this to be you, that is where I come in.

It is now my mission in life to help others realize their untapped potential in life. I am incredibly passionate about bringing people out of the dark and disrupting the normal monotony of life that so many of us have fallen victim to. I do this in casual conversations, with videos I create, social media posts and coaching and or mentoring sessions that I do. I take advantage of any situation I can in order to enlighten someone or at the very least get them thinking from another perspective.

It is often said that *you can lead a horse to the water but you can't make him drink.* To be perfectly clear and transparent with you, I don't work with people who only "kind of want to make a change", or who "sort of would like to achieve more in my life". That's not my niche and I don't have time for it. I only make time for those who are serious about taking their life to the next level, whether that be in their business, career, passion project, or family life. It's pretty easy to tell the difference between those who just want it and those who truly *must* have it. The difference can be seen in how they talk about it but the most telling sign is in their actions. The ones who say they're going to do something but routinely have a self-validated excuse for not getting it done are not committed. Put another way, if the delivered results are always tainted with excuses, there is no true commitment. There are no exceptions to this rule.

I have made the decision in my life to live my passion to the fullest extent. I want to help others discover themselves by defining *their* passions, letting go of their past and taking massive action. I not only say this on a daily basis but I also practice it, actively, on a daily basis. One of my outcome goals is to provide value to thousands, even millions of people, that will allow them to have a vision for more in life. To do this, I created the company Big Lake Visions, which provides visionary life coaching for those who wish to invest their time towards self-development and maximizing greatness in their lives. I have the incredible privilege to work with some pretty amazing people in this capacity. Watching them work hard at what they want most in life and achieving the goals they set for themselves is truly fulfilling for me. They benefit from the coaching because it gives them the extra push they need in order to reach greatness. I benefit from it because people who are achievers truly inspire me. I also actively engage in public speaking and book writing to provide multiple avenues of learning. This list in not all inclusive and it will continue to grow because that is what I do; I grow. I do this so that I can continue to provide value to others who are in need and have the desire to change.

Jayson Gerald
www.biglakevisions.com
jaysongerald@biglakevisions.com

IGNITION 12

Never Too Young To Help

John R.F. Humphreys

Hi I am John Humphreys, "The Happiness Creator." I wrote the book BE AMAZING A Guide To Becoming The Best Version Of Yourself, to motivate and inspire people of all ages to unleash the best versions of themselves.

I have been fortunate to have had people come up to me and share some of the positive effects that I have had on them from either speaking on stage, working one on one and teaching them something new, through reading BE AMAZING, or by being helpful and making them smile. It feels good to help others.

I believe when people overcome their fears and set their mind toward success anything is possible. I have heard my mentor, Mr. Les Brown, say repeatedly, "You are never too old to learn and never too young to teach." With that said, I think everyone can make a big difference in another person's life, but I feel that sometimes we do not understand the effect we have on the world.

Let me explain with an example. I was speaking with one of my magician friends, Mr. Arlen Zachary, about this very thing just the other day. He told me a story about how one day he was performing magic for some children and soon after he started his show one boy in the front fell asleep and then slept through the whole show. Mr. Arlen felt like he was not doing a good job and wondered what he could have done better to be more entertaining. Later the woman with the boy that fell asleep came up to my friend and said, "Thank you so much." She went on to explain that the boy had been run over by a train and lost both his legs. Since the accident, every time the boy would try to go to sleep he would have bad nightmares and re-live the train accident. It was only when he was relaxed, happy, and felt safe that he was able to sleep peacefully and get rest.

This not only changed my friend's perspective, but also reminded me that you really do not know what someone else is going through. I have heard many other examples of how one kind act helped someone else to continue on or change their path for the better.

A good mentor or coach is able to help you navigate and avoid the pitfalls that so many of us fall into. This is why you want to get a mentor or coach who is doing what you want to be doing, or has done what you want to do, so they know where those pitfalls are.

It is true one of the best teachers is failure. It is not the failure itself, but how you overcome it and get back up. One of my favorite examples of this is Mr. Thomas Edison. Mr. Edison made thousands of unsuccessful attempts at inventing the light bulb. When a reporter asked, "How did it feel to fail thousands of times?" Mr. Edison replied, "I didn't fail thousands of times. I just found 9,999 ways not to make a light bulb." Sometimes things take thousands of steps or tries."

When you listen to people speaking about their own experiences or sharing information that they have learned from others mistakes or success, they are giving you the opportunity to learn from them. The more you learn the more you will know and the more you can do. This is how we can stand on the shoulders of the giants and trailblazers that have gone before us.

With technology and fast-paced lives, it is hard to look back and understand how we have gotten to such a fabulous place. Without looking back and learning from history we cannot create a better future. History has a way of repeating itself time and time again. This is why it is so important to understand what the mistakes are and how to avoid them in the future.

I think if we all just try each day to be a little bit better than the day before the world will be a better place.

When you have the right mindset, you can make a better choice. In life we will always have opportunities, challenges, and choices. When you face these with a positive attitude and a readiness to learn, then you can choose to be better and not bitter.

A child learns through play and faces the day with adventure and optimism. That means a rainy day can be a fun day of jumping in mud puddles. A day at the beach can be a treasure hunt. At some point as people grow up we tend to forget that learning can be fun and everyday can be filled with laughter and happiness. Smiles are contagious, so try to smile more and see how many people smile back at you.

It is important not to judge yourself based on your opinion, but to try to understand that people have different perspectives. Once you understand that every action has a reaction, you can choose what action to take for the desired reaction. In other words, if you put good into the world you will get good back. That doesn't mean it will come wrapped in a bow. It means that if you have a positive attitude you will be able to see by the smiles on other people's faces the positive effect you have. The saying "The more you give, the more you get" is so true.

Stuff happens in life. No matter how happy and positive you are that does not mean you will not have a bad day or lose your job or get sick, but it does mean that when one door closes another door opens. You might have to look for the new door, but it is there. People can be at the same amazing event and react to it differently. Some people live their whole lives in the hope that they can go to Disney World, and other people will go to Disney World, "The Happiest Place On Earth", and find a way to be miserable. The choice is yours.

If you would like to connect with me please visit my JohnJohn360.com website.

John R.F. Humphreys
www.JohnJohn360.com

IGNITION 13

Get Out Of Your Head And Into Your Heart

Kim L. Trosper

Growing up, I was the only child. Although my Mom had 15 brothers and sisters and there were many cousins, I wasn't close to anybody except my grandmother and 1 cousin. My Mom and I never seemed to get along when I was a child and I never knew why. In my world, it was my grandmother that was my mom and I referred to her as Mom also. It wasn't that I had a bad childhood, it was just that Mom always maintained that I had to be "seen and not heard." To me, it meant that that my thoughts and opinions didn't matter and I behaved in ways that I thought would make me the centre of attention. I simply didn't want to be invisible. Others thought my behavior was selfish, seeing as I didn't have to share any of my space or belongings. Some saw me as bratty and the more controlling Mom got the more improved I became at being bratty. It wasn't until I was in my late 20's that I realized that in order to get along with her I would have to tow the line. As soon as I towed my own line, there was drama and conflict.

I graduated from high school at 18 years of age and left home to get married at the age of 19. He was an older man who was very loving and supportive of anything and everything I did or didn't do. Being the selfish brat that I had learned to be all my life, I couldn't keep a job. Every time I was asked to do something I didn't like, I would quit and this became a vicious cycle that my supportive husband encouraged. Since working for someone else wasn't working for me, I decided to sell Real Estate and be my own boss. This meant that I could work as much or as little as I wanted to.

I don't remember how I came across a volunteer position to be a Guardian Ad Litem but I went to court to represent children who were placed in foster care. I loved the idea and completed 6 months of training which changed the trajectory of my life. My heart open up to others and I began to care about people's needs and the selfish brat that I was died. Within one happy year of volunteering I was helping children and feeding homeless people, I decided to open my own home and become a foster parent. Although my husband was reluctant, he agreed to it because it was what I wanted. Our first child was a 2 week-old baby girl who we immediately fell in love with and decided to adopt, so she would never have to leave. Over the next 2 years we had several children come and go and then adopted a 2 day old baby boy whose mother had abandoned him by signing him over to the state. We fell in love with several of the children that graced our home but after 3 years I eventually put a stop to wanting to be a parent to all of them.

By this time, I had been married several years and started to feel that I didn't want to be married to my husband any more. My Mom reminded me about the material losses I would suffer and encouraged me not to abandon my big home, car, boat, financial stability and great husband. She somehow convinced me to stay and against my better judgments I eventually fell pregnant with my own child. I remained married for 6 more years, quiet, unhappy and going through the motions of being a wife and Mom. I eventually found the courage to end my marriage and although I lost all the comforts that I was accustomed to, I was a different person now and I found that my inner joy from being a parent and having peace of mind meant more to me. Dare I say it! My freedom was priceless.

At 33, my inner achiever was shouting at me to get a college degree. My alter ego, the self-critic kept putting me off and told me I couldn't do it. My alter ego told me that my kids needed me to stay home and be there for them. I listened for a long time and eventually listened to my heart. I graduated with a Bachelors degree at age 40. It took me 7 years to do but since the old brat in me was put to sleep, I stayed the course and achieved my dream. Frankly, I have never felt more alive as a result of making the decision to study and achieve my degree on my own steam. The experience has taught me that you are never too old to achieve anything as long as you remain committed to it.

I barely recognize myself now. It has been quite a journey. The humanitarian in me lives on as I continue to do my bit for children, the aged and the homeless. I wouldn't change a thing about my past or present. I love spreading love, light and inspiration all around.

I would like to encourage everyone to get out of their heads and come into their own hearts because when they do they will be able to open their hearts and heads and live the life of their dreams.

Kim L. Trosper
www.kimtrosper.com
kim@kimtrosper.com
001-772-985-1371

IGNITION 14

What Is Time?

Leroy Flemming

We have been told that time is past, present, and future, yet we still seem to behave in the same way. We act as if we have all the time in the world. This was me as it related to my mother. My mother loved her children and tried to educate each one of us the best she could. She imparted many things to me and she always said, "No one lives forever." As a child, I didn't grasp this. As I grew older, people close to me left the earth. I truly didn't understand time or how it related to my life until I went off to college.

One day I was pulled from class by the campus police and told to call my mother. She told me my father had passed away. I was trying to prove to my father that I could do something with my life, but his passing interrupted my journey. I learned time doesn't care about your feelings or your dreams. I was able to complete my degree at Alabama State University because of my mother. When I completed my education, she was excited for me, but I felt empty. I wanted more for her and my family. I wasn't focused on time while all of this was happening. I moved from city to city trying to uncover my dream and it led me to Orlando, Florida. It was here that I would find a way to finally give my mother the things I had always dreamed I would.

January 1st, 2000 my mother left this planet. My past didn't matter, the future didn't make sense, and my present was filled with pain. How was I to cope with this new reality? There is something about time that really shook my foundation. I could listen to whomever I wanted, talk to the most qualified spiritual leaders, read all the books that could reshape my mind, but I couldn't get around the idea of time. It seemed so harsh. Why did time replace my joy with such tremendous pain? Why would time take the ones I loved? Over the years I learned that time is chronologically set to govern our entire world. We all have a purpose, for ourselves, our families, communities, and the world. We're all searching for that one goal to give life its profound meaning. This is when poetry entered my life. This experience forced me to develop a concept called **AA+E.** This concept is a three-step process. Life is a series of events and it must contain exciting times, and moments of silence. It was in these situations I found **AA+E. Acknowledge, Affirm, and Execute.**

Acknowledge – to recognize as genuine or valid. You must acknowledge what you want for yourself. What you want is valid. You can't be clear to others if you're not clear with yourself. this is an internal concept. In this step you don't have to share with anyone. This is your visualization stage. When my mother passed away, I lost myself in the pain. I couldn't eat, sleep, and was mentally lifeless. By grace I got up every day. Then, I began to set my mind on how I could get past this. I wanted to get past her leaving me empty. I had to acknowledge this new reality in my mind. I had to assert it into my life. This led to my next reveal.

Affirm – to show a strong belief in our dedication to something. When you set your mind and focus your mental energy on a goal, you must affirm what you want (remember this is your time and life). You must begin the process of writing out a plan. Outlining the action steps that will move you towards your dreams eliminating any negative thoughts about the goals you have set for yourself. I had the dream of buying my mother a home. All my life was set on this one objective. I could see it in my mind and moving to Orlando was the open door to all that would come true for me. Life and time got in the way. Her death, her life, and my life were all intertwined. I needed to unplug, to heal. I began to write poetry. While writing my mind was releasing emotions that I'd never felt before, feelings that were so deep they pulled tears out of my soul. As I placed words on the page, I was reaffirming my dreams and goals. The pain was subsiding. I was beginning to feel whole again. I was on the right track which brings me to,

Execution – The act of doing or performing something. This is the most crucial step of all. Once you pass the acknowledge stage and affirm what you want **you must act**. No action, No fulfillment! It does not matter how long it takes. My mind started to fill up the pages with phrases. I was trying to heal myself and realized my work had the potential to help others understand who they are. I didn't have any connections in the publishing industry. It seemed so far away. I felt that no matter what I wanted it wouldn't come to pass. I didn't give up and continued to network until I made a connection that led to getting my first book published which led to me publishing nine more. All of them dedicated to my mother. This is what execution can do. If you don't give up, you can reach your dreams and goals. Time is not your friend, nor is time your enemy. Time is just time. Your mind is the past, present, and future, but you can only accomplish what you want in the present. Each day is a step towards your goals. I am still chasing my dream for my mom even though she is gone. I must fulfill it and so should you.

Apply Acknowledge, Affirm, and Execution. With focus and determination, you will get there.

Leroy Flemming
Story edited by Clara Mcclenton
Websites: www.timelightenment.biz and www.soulsplitting.biz
Email: info@timelightenment.com

IGNITION 15

Happiness Is A Choice

Lyn-Dee Eldridge

There are times in our lives when things change. New Chapters begin and many times, we just don't understand how to turn the page in order to create our own happiness in relationships, business or career, health, or a change of address. Sometimes we are not only lost but unsure which direction are we going in. Understanding How To Maintain A Positive Productive Posture While Your Cookies Are Crumbling is the key. You have to believe that everything has purpose! Living in the present and being flexible when change happens is important. Becoming a solutionist and not allowing life to paralyze us is paramount.

Hi, my name is Lyn-Dee Eldridge, The Chief Happiness Officer and Founder of Happiness Jungle LLC. I am an Author, Keynote Speaker, Breast Cancer Survivor, Humorist, Entrepreneur, Certified Co-Brand Partner, Coach, and Mentor with Les Brown. I am also the Creator / Producer / TV personality of The Happiness Jungle TV Show.

In my first book, written in 2009, 'Tears Of Fears Behind Closed Doors', I shared how I came from an abusive upbringing. Being told I was nothing, I will never amount to anything. Physically, mentally, sexually battered. At the age of 18, I married my first husband because he said words to me I have never heard before. I was beautiful, unique, and very special. He won my heart only to abuse me for 8 years. Prince charming turned into anus. The blessing out of this relationship is my beautiful daughter, Sica, who has now blessed me with four beautiful granddaughters. She was my strength and I divorced him when she was 15 months old.

Self-help and Personal Development is my savior. I started investing and believing in myself. Les Brown was the first Motivational Speaker I ever heard. "You Have Greatness Within." Then I heard Jim Rohn, Zig Ziglar and Maya Angelou to name a few more. I attended and still attend live seminars. I have coaches and mentors to continue to develop myself into more greatness. I am present. One challenge for me is I am also dyslexic. My solution is listening to audio's to help me along the way.

I became unstoppable. The world was changing around me because I took ownership of the things I had control over which is myself and what serves me. I learned investing in myself is a spiritual and financial gain. Letting go of what was with appreciation of what is with no regrets, is the cornerstone of living. Being selfish to become selfless isn't evil, its necessary. I learned everything that I wanted would benefit from this. My vocabulary changed from stinking thinking I was a subject of Murphy's Law, to learning not to ask why are my cookies crumbling, but what is the purpose?

During the next 18 years, I became an entrepreneur and a successful business woman with no college degree. I learned I AM enough. I followed my passion to help others because of my story. Showing up from the school of hard knocks, I became a resourceful solutionist. I am always growing. I didn't need anyone else but me. That the world is full of life. I kept moving forward even when I failed. I changed my environment, my mindset and never lost sight of my subconscious actions, words and peers. I was manifesting positivity and things were happening around me that I thought only happened for others. My dreams were coming true.

In 2004, I met a nice guy. I fell in love! Moved to New Hampshire from Florida. Married after 2 years and was with him for almost 13 years. Things weren't working out, however I didn't give up easily and tried so hard to make it work, until it was clear, I was never going to be a priority, I shouldn't stay. I had to let go. It was painful. The difference this time around, I loved myself and knew I deserve to be loved unconditionally by another and until I find that person, it was ok to be alone.

In January of 2017 we separated. I decided to go down to South Florida to visit my abusive 84 year-old mother and to build my new world-wide entity, Happiness Jungle, LLC. That was the plan.

My world shattered as if a tornado hit me. My cookies were crumbling all around me.

My mother became very sick. I became her caretaker, putting my life and business on pause for almost one year. I have two older siblings and it was very clear they weren't showing up to help. I canceled twenty paid speaking engagements. Then on September 26th, 2017, I was told Breast Cancer invaded my ta-ta's. While going through surgery and radiation, I divorced and had to file for bankruptcy.

You're probably thinking, WOW! This would throw anyone into a deep depression. However, I am happy to share with you I wouldn't allow this to happen to me. I thought immediately, what is the purpose? I now share my stories to help others grow and step into their happiness and greatness! I am determined to thrive on every opportunity I am presented with. How? By teaching others how to;

- Let go of what you have no control over. Les Brown said, "It's not your responsibility to make others happy."

- Give yourself permission to move on. Jim Rohn said, "Your life does not get better by chance, it gets better by change." "Happiness is not something you postpone for the future; it is something you design for the present."

- Forgiveness is a master key. Forgiveness will set you free. Zig Ziglar said, "When you forgive somebody else you accept the responsibility for your own future"

- Rise above it all. Maya Angelou said, "You may shoot me with your words, you may cut me with your eyes, you may kill me with your hatefulness, but still, like air, I'll rise!"

When your cookies crumble like mine have; cancer, abuse, divorce, grieving, single-parenting, co-parenting, step-parenting, becoming a care-taker, business owner, and dealing with financial pressures, aka, bankruptcy, you can learn how to work through everything with a happier, more positive attitude and purpose. I have been able to scale, measure and add value by turning all my cookie crumbs into opportunities for growth and empowerment.

"I never said life was easy, but I did say you can be happier. You were born to shine, hold your own flashlight!"

Lyn-Dee Eldridge
www.happinessjungle.com
Lyn-Dee@happinessjungle.com
001-603-660-6010

IGNITION 16

To Be Or Not To Be

Manju Chhabra

"Khudi ko kar buland itna ke har taqdeer se pehle khuda bande se khud pooche bata teri raza kya hai."- *Muhammad Iqbal Translation: "When you focus on being a blessing, God makes sure that you are always blessed. Strive for others and the divine will grace you."*

These words are at the centre of my belief system and whatever I pursue, they are aligned directly to the philosophy of Muhammad Iqbal Saheb.

Being ready to help and add value to other's work is something I have always wanted to do. As a result, I have always directed a lot of my energy to this type of work and I am at my happiest and most energetic when I am doing this. It is, in fact, my greatest joy and pleasure.

I was raised in the kind of household that placed more importance on discipline than open communication and love. By the time I reached my teen years, responsibility was second nature and though

I wasn't happy taking care of an entire household at that age, including taking care of my ailing grandmother, it prepared me for so much more than most children my age could handle. My teacher and coach Les Brown has always said that if you take responsibility for yourself you will develop a hunger to accomplish your dreams. On hindsight, whilst I went through the motions of being responsible for the household, I was also inadvertently nurturing dreams that I had the burning desire to accomplish. It was inevitable that I would!

My responsibilities soon extended into the family business and whilst I maintained the reigns there, I also nurtured the side of me that enjoyed counseling and advising and I took great pleasure in doing these for friends and colleagues. Under my leadership, the business prospered, taking many awards and though this gave me great pleasure, I also still secretly nurtured the dream of doing what my heart wanted me to.

"Maybe the journey isn't so much about becoming anything. Maybe it's about unbecoming everything that isn't really you, so you can be who you were meant to be in the first place."-unknown.

My calling was to help people to rise up from their struggles and I soon realized that I had to take the responsibility for going forward on my own rather than waiting for opportunities to knock at my door. I furthered my studies to include counseling and coaching and though this was challenging, it was satisfying. Watching others and being a part of empowering, uplifting, improving and elevating the lives of others who were at a point of no return, was simply so gratifying. You know you are doing the right thing when what you do brings a smile to your face, a twinkle to your eyes and a sighed contentment to your heart. I spread my wings and started conducting workshops and so my happiness with what I was doing multiplied.

My empowering workshops included making a shift from victim mentality to leader mentality and my team and I work hard at changing mindsets and attitudes. We try to restore confidence and self- belief in those who have lost it and we teach people to do the same for others so that we can multiply what we do through them. We have successfully done parent and student workshops and have successfully got them to engage with one another, improve their understanding and relationships and above all live in harmony with one another. I have had many "aha" moments and I am grateful for them because they are my greatest joy.

My work has extended to caregivers at old age homes and we work tirelessly to promote proper care, love and compassion for those who are entrusted to care for them. My focus is on helping them to recognize what a vital role they play in the fragile lives of elderly citizens and to make them aware of the nobility in the work that they do. Through that I have been able to facilitate changes in the way the elderly are cared for these days. My work also extends to those injured in wars and those women who are widowed as a result of having soldiers for husbands. This is an extension of my Dads legacy and I feel grateful for being able to extend my own work here.

To make the shift from a distributorship to a coaching and mentoring business which impacts positively on the lives of thousands, took solid self belief, courage, commitment, trust, good intentions, determination and rock solid surety that I would make it successful. Like everyone, I had moments of doubt and suffered setbacks but learned that comebacks are possible and that there is joy in that also.

I have learned that I need to continue learning. Whether that's in a classroom or out in the trenches, I learn and use what I learn to help others successfully.

I have also learned not to compare my life with the lives of others. It's a waste of time and energy because each of us comes to the earth with a purpose 2of our own.

I learned that every new day is a new story in the book of my life and that it is up to me to make every story a good one. I try to teach the same to my daughter and hope that she too will carry my legacy forward, no matter what she chooses to do.

Finally, I believe that every one of us on the earth is a blessing and that if we live life as Muhammad Iqbal suggests, we can all make and leave this world, a little bit better than it was yesterday.

Manju Chhabra
http://www.cactuslilyconsulting.com
Cactuslilyconsulting@gmail.com

IGNITION 17

Change Your Attitude, Change Your Life

Mark Jarema

Change your attitude, change your life. I'll never forget those words that a courageous friend told me a little over 10 years ago. When I hit rock bottom in my life, my friend told me I didn't have a life problem, I had an attitude problem. When he told me that, I was a little offended. He explained to me that sometimes good is not good enough. He wanted me to think about what he told me for a couple of days and if I was willing to try to have an open mind, he was willing to work with me.

I did some internal reflecting and realized I needed his help. I literally had nothing to lose. I knew if I wanted my life to change, I needed to master my attitude. I called him back and was at his mercy. For several months, I listened to every word he said and didn't doubt the process.

At one point in my life, I was at the top of the mountain. I was a director leading a global training team, making a lot of money and traveling the world. I purchased a house, renovated it into a model home, had new vehicles, ate out at nice restaurants almost every night, and was in love with a beautiful woman. Many, including myself, thought I had the perfect life.

And then, in a very short period, I tumbled from the top of the mountain to below sea level. It seemed like overnight that my life turned into a nightmare. I lost all my money, my house was foreclosed and I lost my job. I was sued by a financial institution for an unpaid loan and to top it all, I was diagnosed with a unique type of cancer, and my girlfriend left me.

I became a volunteer victim. I was blaming everyone and complaining about everything. I even blamed God. I didn't want to take responsibility for my life. I mentally moved into victimhood. I let my struggles become my standards.
I went on a journey to study the importance of how your attitude can affect the quality of your life. The first thing I learned is that everything starts with mastering a great attitude. For each level you improve your attitude, you will improve your life just as much. If your attitude is good, make it great. If your attitude is great, make it unforgettable. You can always take your attitude to the next level, no matter how good or great you think it already is.

Everything in life leads back to your attitude. According to Zig Ziglar, "Your attitude, not your aptitude, determines your altitude," meaning how successful and fulfilled you feel in your life is dependent on your attitude. Your attitude is either leading the way, or it's in the way; either connecting you or disconnecting you; either working for you or against you; either helping you or hurting you.

There are two very important concepts to remember about your attitude. The first important thing to keep in mind is that only you can choose your attitude. Nobody else can make the choice of what attitude you wear for the day. The second thing is that your attitude teaches others how you want to be treated. Those who have a great attitude send out a positive signal and others will want to help, work for, and support them. The reverse is true as well. People will shy away, ignore, or even run from people with a negative attitude.

The one thing that can change your life in an instant is mastering your attitude. If you truly want to reach the power of positive thinking, your attitude must be positive. I have never met anyone with a negative attitude who is a positive thinker. I applied this one simple concept to my life and noticed in a very short time that the more I worked on improving my attitude, the more my life started to improve.

Unfortunately, we all know people who have a negative attitude. The frustrating thing about those with a negative attitude is that they're in denial and the last to know they have a negative attitude. I refer to this as stinkin'-thinkin'. It's used to describe self-destructive thought processes and self-doubt. Such thinking can cripple the human spirit. It can lead to depression and stop people from getting the most out of their lives.

Often people will act out in a negative way (unknowingly) when they are dealing with something they don't want to confront. It could be something they are struggling with such as finances, relationships, health, or their self-image. Negative people frequently project their negative attitude onto others, which reflects how they are feeling internally.

To master your attitude takes some soul searching and asking yourself where your attitude ranks daily. Could it be better? You must look in the mirror and mentally expose yourself. You must be willing to be emotionally buck naked to realize there is room for improvement. Without being honest with yourself, chances are, you will remain complacent in life. Self-honesty is too many times underrated, but it's a critical pillar to moving ahead. While being honest with yourself takes courage, avoid being too critical of yourself to the point that it demotivates you. Self-honesty and self-discovery are about knowing, learning, and improving.

You have an attitude toward everything important in your life, such as your health, wealth, career, and relationships. Your attitude toward each of those things will determine the decisions you make, which will determine your outcome. You can look at someone who is fit and know what their attitude is toward their health. They obviously have a great attitude for being healthy, and therefore make better eating choices and exercise on a regular basis; that's why they look fit and healthy. The same is true for your relationships. If your attitude is great toward your relationships, you will make better choices and reap the rewards of meaningful friendships. Your attitude determines your choices, which deliver your outcomes. If you want better outcomes, make better choices; to make better choices, master having a great attitude.

The one common denominator I have observed that separates those who have reached success, lived their dreams, and are fulfilled in life from those always wishing for success was their attitude. Are you a pretender or a contender? Contenders work daily on their attitude and have acute awareness when it needs to improve. Pretenders think their attitude is good enough.

Improving my attitude has changed my life. In the past few years, I have delivered speeches to thousands of people on how to change their lives by using the art of positive thinking and improving their attitude. I have a coaching practice and authored a book; Hit Your Mark & Live The Life You Love. If I can do it....you can too. I'll see you at the top, or from the top.

Mark Jarema
www.jarema.team
mark@jarema.team

IGNITION 18

Dreams In A Briefcase

Michelle Mueller

When i was a little girl, I wanted to be a lawyer. I even pretended I was a lawyer. I would walk around the house with my mother's leather purse and pretend it was my briefcase. That was as close as I got to achieving my dream. My dreams soon got stolen away from me when I became the victim of sexual abuse. Low self esteem kicked in. I turned to drugs and eventually prostitution. My shame and unworthiness soon took over and I became homeless. For 24 long years I let myself live in the darkness of unworthiness because I convinced myself that I didn't care and never mattered. I even allowed myself to be abused and thought that I deserved the hiding that I got. I was in a deep dark space and it seemed that light would never enter my life ever again.

.

I may not have gone to Law school but today I'd like to think of myself as the biggest advocate for homelessness, domestic violence and abandoned women. My purpose is to help as many abandoned women as possible and to give them literal dignity by way of clothing, snacks, hygiene packs and whatever is needed. I believe that every time I do this the advocate in me is saying, "I object!"

I live in a city where the freeway ends, literally and begins with a beach and whilst that is beautiful, it is marred by the hundreds of women who end up here , lonely and vulnerable, with nowhere to go. That cut in the road so literally represents their dead end in life and the ocean so literally swallows up their hope and faith for a better life. People like me are the only way they sometimes get to survive. I try to make life as special as possible for the homeless. I do small things like leave them notes and affirmations and I bring them treats that are unique to their tastes. No, it isn't just a charity exercise. It's a recognition of each ones identity and I firmly believe that everyone deserves to be treated this way.

You can find me in a kitchen cooking and serving alongside my volunteers at the luncheon I sponsor for 75 people in my community. These people have AIDS and for most of them , this is their 1st hot meal they have had all month. Medicine maybe keeping them well, but their hearts crave the love and acceptance I give.

You will soon find me in the city and county jails speaking to female inmates who, in my eyes, are being held prisoners by their own lack of self esteem and fears that a better future are just not within their reach. I will be teaching them how to have healthy relationships with themselves.

Like me, I want to see all the women who have walked in my shoes, lead lives of acceptance and love for themselves. I would like to see them use their experiences to uplift and elevate other women walking the path in as short a time as possible. 24 years was a lot of time to lose on the streets and I don't want that for others.

Today, I am a Les Brown Certified speaker, trainer and coach, sharing my story to help as many victims of abuse, drug and domestic violence and self-sabotage. Encouraging women to speak up, lift each other up high and tear down our walls of fear. I speak and tell women that it is never to late to start over. I did it at 44 years old and that they can be their own boss and own their business. Women need to know that they aren't alone and that they need not suffer in silence.

I believe that God didn't create any spare women. We all have a purpose. Our circumstances may vary but our purposes come together beautifully making us all connect as we were designed to do. We are one. Once we introduce ourselves to ourselves, we can introduce ourselves to the world. Once we love ourselves, we can love one another. Remember, LOVE is a verb and it means that we have to take action in reaching out and helping others through that love. I am not interested in competing, I hope we all win !

I am the founder of the One Red Shoe Foundation and my mission is "There are NO spare women, only women with purpose."

Michelle Mueller
Founder of :One Red Shoe Foundation
www.facebook.com/1redshoe
www.Nosparewomen.com
To donate www.paypal.me/oneredshoe

IGNITION 19

How I Ignited The Champion Within
And Inspired Others To Begin

Nasreen Variyawa

Sometimes there is just so much more wrong than right with you. Sometimes so much more just goes wrong with your life than the right things do. Sometimes there is just so much more weighing against you than for you. Sometimes it's easier to make that your reality and use it to do nothing and to be nothing. That would have been MY story had I not had enough self-worth to recognize that my purpose was to help people and that I could teach them to do that if I just knew enough about how to do it.

The only thing I ever wanted to be in my formative years was a teacher. Even as a student, I helped my class friends to learn lessons they didn't understand. I understood the power of teaching for myself very early on in my life because through it I stopped having to learn so hard. The more I taught my classmates the better I understood each subject. Although I graduated with excellent results from high school I did not go to teacher training college. Through circumstances beyond my control, my life took a small

71

but life altering detour and I lived some of toughest days of my life. It was character building and though I survived I faced health, financial, social and other challenges I wasn't prepared for. Days were rough and my future appeared bleak but I persevered.

Fate smiled at me when I bagged a job at a leading distance education institution as a dispatch clerk. Surrounded by academic professionals, I dreamed of the day I too would be able to deliver a lecture or write a book. I resolved to learn from every source available as I explored everything from minute taking and strategic management to dissertation writing, event management and travel. I said yes to every instruction, learnt how to do it afterwards and then taught the same to others after mastering the science myself. I began formal studies in the education field and steadily built skills in training, coaching, mentoring, skills development facilitation, assessment, moderation and public speaking until I achieved my first Diploma in the field.

I later got headhunted by big education brands and started writing learner guides for colleges and training departments. I lapped it all up as I gained momentum leading in the field and achieving better things every year. The accolades poured in. However, success wasn't in my accolades. They were in the first letters written home by gold and diamond miners who learnt to read and write from me. They were in the many learners who said they couldn't but eventually did. They were in the many aspiring teachers and trainers who turned out to be better than I ever was. They were and still are in the many students and colleagues who get in touch from time to time to tell me where they applied what I taught them and how they are doing right now. There is no better feeling than that for it is in their accomplishments that I see my own success.

Wanderlust soon grabbed my attention so I did a quick TESOL programme and enrolled for a Post- Graduate Diploma in

Education Leadership and Management. Unstopped, I loaded my books into my suitcase and travelled to teach English in Turkey. Brave, I went against the grain and taught in schools in the East of Turkey where the possibility of terrorist attacks hangs over your head like an axe but where people respect and hold education in such high esteem. Nothing was sweeter than going home to graduate at the very University I helped establish and receive my diploma from the very professors who were my mentors when I worked as a junior clerk.

Many see my role as an English teacher as a step down from the ladder I appeared to be climbing rapidly. I don't see it that way. I maybe teaching English to children but I use my coaching and mentoring skills to affect their lives in ways that I hope are positive. They may understand very little of what I teach daily but I feel the impact when I observe them demonstrate love, kindness, respect and a can do attitude to difficult things.

Through online coaching and mentoring, I have been able to network with people who have a similar mindset. Together, we influence people to set goals and go after them step by step. Then we teach them the importance of doing the same for others so that the circle of light, empowerment and upliftment is spread far and wide.

I have been blessed with the gift of writing and through 3 published works on Kindle have been able to teach people to lead themselves and others, to understand the power of love in all things that they do and how to ignite the champion within and inspire others to begin. I consider the ability to have written these books amongst my biggest blessings because they are the legacy through which I will live long after I am gone.

I have always believed in the power of teaching and to this end I once wrote, "1 thought, 1 vision, 1 book, 1 dream, 1 willing student and 1 willing teacher can change your entire world. Whether you are the willing student or the willing teacher or both, your world changes for the better, irrespective." My whole life and career are the cornerstone of teaching and whenever I want to remember my WHY, these words in which my belief is etched, remind me that my role is unequivocally the most powerful yet most humbling and most loving in the world.

Challenges are a given. They will come and go and sometimes they will leave a little damage but remember that it's when the damage is at its worst or when your life is at its darkest , that you must nurture your dreams and goals. They hold the power to keep you together and give you a reason to keep yourself intact. Just as when you have lost your spouse and you are told to be strong for your children so too when your world is falling apart, you must tell yourself to keep strong for your dreams. They are, after all, the children that you must live to nurture.

Anything and everything you want to achieve in your life depends on your ability to lead yourself. Remember that just like all leadership begins with self-leadership so too must you ignite the champion within before you can ever inspire others to begin.

Keep smiling, keep shining, keep rising

Nasreen Variyawa
https://nvariyawa.wixsite.com/nasreenv
www.facebook.com/Ignitify/
nvariyawa@yahoo.com

IGNITION 20

Step Into Your Greatness

Dr Patrick Businge

I was not born in the greatness of Great Britain but in the poverty of Uganda. Although, I lived there during the war, I did not let war live in me. I remember that on one night when we had just finished our dinner, we were preparing to sleep. Suddenly, there were noises and gunshots outside. Running out for safety, my family and I ran into the banana plantations and spent the night there. When we came back in the morning, a large part of our house was destroyed, my parent's shop had been burgled, and my primary school had been turned into an army barracks. I remember having to travel in a refugee truck to a new village where our lives resumed, but was never the same again.

Under these circumstances, I could never have ever imagined that I would study in 7 Universities and gain over 7 university qualifications. I could have never imagined that I would go on to create my own university and help people step into their greatness. So, what made the difference? It's really very simple, having education.

I did not let my circumstances derail my dreams for a better future. I always maintained that war wasn't a permanent condition. I rose above my circumstances and made greatness my benchmark. So I let my belief drive my conviction in education. Education helped me realise that though I lived in war, I should not let war live in me. Education helped me to understand that though I lived in poverty, I should not let poverty live in me. Education helped me realise that both poverty and war were not permanent. I did not let war kill my dream of studying in a world class university like Cambridge. It fuelled me to walk many miles to school barefoot and work in plantations under the heat of the sun to raise money for my school fees. My dream was finally realised when I completed my PhD from Exeter University, one of the finest universities in the world.

I am now an educator and have taught over 50,000 people in classrooms, churches, orphanages, villages, community centres, and boardrooms throughout the United Kingdom, Europe, Africa, and the Americas. I am a strong believer in lifelong learning and personal development. Living in a world characterised by war, plagued by a shortage of hope and marred with average performance, my ultimate vision is to inspire one million people to become instruments of peace, messengers of hope and channels of greatness. I do this through the university I created, Greatness University: world's first institution dedicated to discovering, unlocking, and monetising greatness in individuals and businesses.

Through my work at Greatness University, I help people escape physical, mental and moral poverty through education. At Greatness University, we believe that greatness leaves clues. We are therefore committed to helping people like you tap into their greatness faster and easily than you can ever imagine. We do this by researching what makes people great, organizations flourish, and businesses thrive. We find out what drives people to become great in all spheres of life. We help people create their personal economies by monetising their greatness. We guide people on the best ways to create lasting legacies. We work daily and tirelessly so that the people we love are also left with lasting legacies of greatness that we hope will live on long after they are gone.

The civil rights activist, singer and author Maya Angelou says, 'There is no greater agony than bearing an **untold story** inside you'. I believe you have an untold story within you. Your story does not need to go unheard. Your story needs to be written and spoken so that whoever reads or listens to it can say, 'It is because of you, I did not give up on life'.

In effect, I help people discover, develop and deliver their stories. As a Book Creation Coach, my team and I run retreats on how to discover, write, publish and monetise books. I myself have authored 7 published works and it gives me immense pleasure to know that they have been well received by the public and other authors as well. It gives me immense satisfaction that these books are helping me achieve my goal of creating enough other greatness leaders who will carry the legacy forward.

I not only help people write their stories but I also give them the opportunity to co-author with me and share their stories on Greatness TV where I host the new and popular show *You Changed My Life*. In less than 3 months, I have hosted over 20 guests and co-authors. Again, it gives me immense satisfaction that through the examples of others, I can encourage others to do the kind of work that motivates and inspires them to create their best lives. There is greatness in you. I look forwards to helping you discover your greatness and create your best life.

Dr Patrick Businge
www.patrickbusinge.com

IGNITION 21

Magical Conversations

Dr Pauline Crawford-Omps

As children, a lot of what we can naturally do sets us up for what we can innately do as adults. When I look back on my life back then, I am convinced of this because I had friends coming to me – boys and girls – asking me questions about this and that and wanting my opinions. Girlfriends wanted my advice on boys, and the boys were always asking for advice on girls. It was as though they felt I could *magically* tell them what they needed to know. I didn't realise it at the time, but all those elements were gently nudging me to choose the path where all my experiences – internal as well as external – eventually led me.

I help people learn *who* they are. Of greater importance, however, is the nature of my involvement. I work with people to help them learn *why they are who they are*. I know that may sound a little convoluted, but it really isn't. In fact, it was my personal journey down this path ... *discovering why I was who I was* ... that helped me discover my passion to bring what I learned to everybody wanting to find the answer to the truly big questions in life that starts with ... WHY?

It's amazing how much a person can learn through the simple and basic act of observation. It was through observation that I was able to see the variations and individual differences that make each of us unique ... that make you, for example, stand out even in a crowd. Why? Because each of us has some very distinct characteristics, some of which may even mandate, to a degree, certain feelings and the way we express those feelings particularly as we begin to gently – or in some cases perhaps not too gently – add love, and the emotions generated by this key sensation, to the mix. Let me reiterate, at this point, that I know this through first-hand experience.

As a teenage girl I was perhaps more than a little awkward when it came to dealing with the fears, emotions, feelings core to being a teenager; issues that were constantly invading my *safe space* during this period in my social development. I didn't know any more than any other girl or boy my age, and I'm pretty sure this was what compelled to me to develop a look and demeanour that told my peers, "Am I bothered?" Apparently, the message that I inadvertently communicated was, "I know how to cope because I have already figured it out." In retrospect, I think this somewhat dismissive and cavalier attitude that I was able to successfully convey, initiated my introduction to the world of people seeking greater understanding not only of the world, but of themselves.

As a proud and lively baby boomer, I have today, had many adventures across the world. I met my husband - an American musician and educator - in Budapest, Hungary in late 2011 at a conference neither of us wanted to attend. We were aged 62 and 67 respectively, and had it not been for our love of travel and adventure, that would never have happened. Building on the result of our *Magical Conversation* during that conference meeting, we would never have been married at a wedding chapel in Las Vegas, Nevada with an Elvis Presley impersonator singing at the ceremony.

Since then we have continued our travels, circumnavigating the globe in the process. In addition to the countries that each of us has experienced, we lived in Malaysia from 2014 through 2017 when we relocated to the United States, taking up residency in Southern California.

The lessons I learned then and now - my transition from housewife to entrepreneur to educator to international speaker – have helped provide value for clients across the world. People are people everywhere and many issues are the same no matter the cultural overlay. What changes is a person's intention and willingness to grow.

I have personally evolved over my lifetime, and my experiences continue to drive the changes that I have yet to go through. Core to all my work is *The Value Creation Cycle*. It's a relatively straightforward cycle that influences my whole life. It functions on the premise that only *you* can create *your* value. The *'me'* factor is key, because I teach my clients to be open-minded and take a long and very objective look in the mirror … literally.

As awareness grows … and it will … the individual will begin to smile and value their physicality, their biology and their cerebral preferences. They will recognise their natural personality and talents will begin to blossom as they further realise their capacity to add value to relationships and to their life. The 'me' influences the 'you and me' (relationships) and gains momentum for the last part of the cycle, the 'we' impact on their community life. The value cycle creates the understanding that you are responsible for all things in your life. Overtime the magic of life evolves with you in the driver's seat. As my life adventure has evolved, I have become known as *Miss Magical Conversations*!

Valuing our differences as men and women is key to getting along better and co-creating new rules that resolve conflicts without a fight. I have always been passionate about connecting people through conversations that make a difference. Men and women *creating solutions together* is my vision for the future now. I have set a vision for a *Magical Conversation TV Channel* to enable women to listen to the wisdom of men and vice versa. My purpose is to help male leaders to resolve the growing demands of the business landscape where gender mix, the rise of professional career women, the generational merger and cultural awareness are all keys to sustainable success for them and their company. I facilitate behavioural transformation programs that impact people's personal and professional success. I have designed and delivered hundreds of workshops and seminar programs, online and offline, in corporate UK, Asia Pacific and US.

Dr Pauline Crawford-Omps
www.missmagicalconversations.com
www.pauline-crawford-omps.com
www.corporateheart.co.uk
www.genderdynamicsdna.com

IGNITION 22

To Be Successful, Be Happy

Rich Fontaine

Earl Nightingale, one of the Godfathers to 'success teachings' claimed it to be "The progressive realization of a worthy ideal." This means having a goal of an ideal situation and working steadily every day to achieve it.

Now, if this is the definition of success, what in turn would be the meaning of failure? For me, it is to have no ideal goals that I am moving toward and following the crowd. It is doing what everyone else is doing because everyone else is doing it. This is a tremendous path to failure.

Earl Nightingale also said, "The opposite of success is not failure, it's conformity." Doing what everyone else is doing without reason, without question or without drive is the reason most people fail in life.

For many years, I was aimless toward my own goals and purpose. My father instilled that I need an Education. He never said, education would make me happy but thought it was important I had one. My mother drilled in to my subconscious that I should get a safe government job. Again, it may not make me happy, but I needed it. My peers told me to follow trends, my schools taught me to sit down in my seat and be seen but not heard, while the church taught me to be selfless and think of myself last and others first. Again, this did not promote happiness but I did them all.

Doing the "right" thing to make others happy, will not make you happy. I went to the University like my father wanted but he was upset on my graduation day because it took me 7 years instead of 4 years to complete my degree. I got a safe job that my mother wanted and ended up being fired. I sat down in my seat and stayed quiet like the teachers wanted but as I got older I got called it anti-social. I was selfless like the church wanted and spent more energy on other people but then I was giving more that I was receiving. Even when I followed the trends like my peers wanted, I became outdated too often.

It wasn't until I started thinking, doing and being how I wanted to be that I found success and happiness. I used a few ways to do this and that is what I want to share with you.

- **My thoughts are important**: In the Book of God it is said, "As a man thinketh, in his heart, so he is." I understood from this that how I thought would reflect how I became. So, I did just that. I adjusted the way I thought about people, listened to others I looked up to and changed my thoughts positively about love, harmony, prosperity, gratitude, abundance, happiness and expensive things. "An idle mind is the Devil's workshop." So, I took control of my thoughts and negative habits and gravitated towards a more focused life which paid back the dividends.

83

- **Whatever I give, I receive:** Once I could get my thoughts under control, I began giving what I wanted to receive. I wanted to see nicer people in the world, so the more I smiled the more I received it. Now, even if you're positive, you will always meet your opposition. The point is to stay on your high level and not to revert down to theirs. Even if someone is rude, share the blessing of being kind and you will reap kindness in return. I therefore understood that if I wanted to attract abundance I had to give off myself and I did. I started to see the money, kindness, motivation, free content in studies, encouragement and all sorts of good things started to happen to me. I firmly that whatever you give in goodwill you will get back into your life tenfold.

- **Create Success Habits:** How you do one thing, is how you do everything. If you give a half-hearted effort on one front, it usually shows its self on another. I realized that if I wanted to strive for excellence, I had to do be excellent at whatever I was doing. In my health, I didn't just want to be healthy, I wanted to be incredibly healthy, in my mind, body and soul. In career, I just did not want an ok career, I wanted a phenomenal career. In my finances, I did not want average finances, I wanted abundance. I did not want a sub-par relationship, I wanted the most loving relationship I could imagine. In saying that, if I wanted to achieve these things, I had to create the habit of having these things in my life. So, I put effort into all these aspects in which I wanted to excel and sure enough success in these areas followed naturally.

Finally, I consider the opportunity to share all the information I do as a blessing. It brings great goodwill, love and blessings and that to me is success. I get to share the stage with Les Brown quite often or write books that help motivate and improve the lives of others all over the world. I get to teach courses about how to be successful and how to write and grow rich and that is also a blessing I get to share with the world. I get to share my vision and purpose with everyone in the hope that it will others do the same things I have done and be happy because I truly believe that to be successful, happiness is a must.

Rich Fontaine
www.powerofselfent.com
powerofselfentertainment@gmail.com

IGNITION 23

If You Feed Your Faith,
Your Doubts Will Starve To Death

Shasni Afsal

Miracles and magic happen every day, and it happened in my life at the age of 29. By then I had become a wife, and a mother of two kids, and I had even forgotten that I ever had a dream of becoming a singer.

I'm Shasni Afsal, from Kerala, India. During my childhood, my favourite pastime was listening to songs and singing them. For as long as I can remember, I would spend hours listening to songs, imbibing what I was listening to, quietly preparing myself for the talent that would one day, break through.

My father, being an educationalist, never encouraged my singing, as he always wanted me to study and secure an esteemed job. I loved my father dearly and looked up to him, so I crushed the spirit for singing within me partly out of not wanting to disappoint him and partly because I believed he knew what was best for me.

As fate would have it, the opportunities to sing in school and college would keep popping up despite a lack of any attempt I would make to conceal my talent. You can imagine the battle between my head and heart when every time I was felicitated for my singing I quelled the urge to pursue it. The battle between head and heart continued and I lost interest in my studies and I ended up pursuing English studies after school.

I married just after my Degree and enrolled for post graduation and it was my husband who sent me to music school but I couldn't continue because so many things were happening in my life. Again, I suppressed my passion for music and I buried myself in taking care of my marriage and my family.

In 2011, we moved to Abu Dhabi (UAE) and I buried myself into adjusting into a new life there. When we completely surrender ourselves to our Creator, He opens the doors that no one can close, and sends help out of nowhere. In 2015, mum who missed me terribly asked me to send her a few songs by voice note. İ did it just to please her. Unbeknown to me, she shared the clips and I began receiving offers for albums. People in the music business were finally knocking at my door. I got opportunities to sing in albums with leading playback singers and started getting great response to my songs.

I finally found what made me feel alive and happy again and though it has not been a cakewalk, it has made me stronger and more ready to deal with life's challenges. Now, no matter what challenges I face, I face them bravely because my soul feels renewed and uplifted from being able to sing again. I have stopped worrying about external approval and have begun to focus only on making good music.

The main issue I face is the wearing of hijab (head scarf) and I suppose the image I project does not fit into the mainstream image of most people in the industry. But I am very clear in heart and mind that my talent and objectives are aligned and that I don't see the need for my hijab to affect my albums, performances or appearances in stage shows. For me, the definition of freedom is being able to make your own choices, without hurting other's sentiments. I just want to be myself and the phrase, "take me as I am or not at all" applies to me right now in my life.

Things have gotten slightly better since I first burst onto the scene and I have made a lot more appearances on You Tube, some TV shows and other platforms. I am honestly enjoying this phase because it is a phase in which I have shed inhibitions and have begun to experiment more with styles, languages and even content.

My journey has taught me 3 distinct lessons which I want to share with the readers. I feel very strongly that if I didn't share these that a lot of others walking in my shoes or facing other challenges would be left demotivated and uninspired.

The first lesson is that you should believe in yourself and pursue your dreams. You never have to be disrespectful to anyone when they refuse to support your dreams, but you do have to be assertive enough to stand your ground and find ways to realize your goals. Believe in yourself!

The second lesson is that not everyone has to like you or what you do or what you wear or the choices you make. You have to like yourself and you have to be happy with yourself first before others can be happy with you.

The last lesson I will share with you is that you ought to be grateful to your Creator irrespective of whether you are in favorable or unfavorable conditions. Gratitude to Him is invaluable and I think faith in Him is priceless. There is no point in becoming depressed over things that we cannot control anymore. We should be grateful for what we still have and focus on what we still can do. There is only value in talking to your Creator and trusting that He will find a way for you.

Following my bliss transformed me into a more confident, better, and a happier person who understands and respects the value of gratitude. My vision is backed by a mission. I want my fellow homemakers to be aware that it's never too late to dream big. Having a family doesn't mean that we should give up on our dreams. I want them to understand that we are powerful enough to transform our lives by shifting our focus from negative to positive and manifesting our dreams into reality. We should not waste anymore time worrying, overthinking or doubting ourselves. Remember, life gets better only when we get better.

Shasni Afsal
shasniafsal1@gmail.com
YouTube:
https://www.youtube.com/channel/UC3Xrg09OHzxZWYessSe88
7g
www.facebook.com/shasni.afsal

IGNITION 24

Short-Term Pain, Long-Term Gain

Shaweta "Shay" Vasudeva

"ShayTheCoach" is a company that I founded as a result of my passion to help others become the best version of themselves. Under STC, I offer one-on-one sessions using Corrective Exercise, Nutritional Coaching, and Cranial Sacral Work at my Phoenix location. I believe that one size does NOT fit all, and work with clients during their initial session to create a plan of action. Together, we decide which services will be the best fit and adjust them over time, as clients reach their goals and experience positive results.

I grew up as a competitive athlete, playing national level softball and tennis. I also started training martial arts at the age of 10. By the time I was in college, I had a multitude of injuries and health conditions. These injuries left me physically and emotionally depleted. Even after a traumatic incident that resulted in a dislocated wrist, I chose to continue to play. As a result, I ended up needing a major surgery on my wrist. I was in a cast for almost one year and physical therapy for multiple years. I was on an emotional low and was prescribed medication for pain. I started eating food for emotional gratification. The result of my poor eating habits and a sedentary lifestyle was enormous weight gain.

By 22, I was close to a 160 pounds but once my cast came off, my determination kicked in and I began to retrain with Sensei (karate instructor). I eventually earned the rank of Black Belt which was a very gratifying and a life-changing achievement. Along with my karate training, I studied extensively and earned an Associate Degree in Applied Science (Alcohol and Substance Use Disorders), and a Bachelor and Master of Arts in Psychology. I didn't stop there. I also earned my Certified Personal Trainer and Corrective Exercise Specialist credentials from the National Academy of Sports Medicine and am a Certified Nutritional Therapist from The Health Sciences Academy. I'm currently working towards a Master of Science Degree in Kinesiology from A.T. Still University.

I enjoy working with pre- and post-retirees, working adult professionals, people with weight loss goals, folks who have muscle imbalances from overuse/repetitive movements, and people on ketogenic diets.

I am also a teaching professional, speaker, and author. I enjoy working with small teams and large groups alike. I am known for my unique approach where I combine education with application. I believe providing education is invaluable during STC sessions and I pair it with a dynamic approach to help clients put what they learn into practice. In other words, I focus on helping others apply what they learn in their sessions. I use a Mind-Body, integrated approach in my sessions and workshops, bringing 15+ years of combined experience in Psychology, Personal Training, Corrective Exercise, Nutrition, and Martial Arts to my style.

One of my mentors told me that in business, you either grow or you go. I feel that way about life too. When things get bumpy we ought to utilize the opportunities for growth. For example, I didn't always enjoy my current level of health or look like I do. Through my own personal weight loss and transformative health journey, I have come to believe that the best knowledge and experience comes from working with others and studying, always striving to do better today than I did yesterday.

I've also done my bit as a Drug and Alcohol Counselor, working with individuals, families, and couples to recover from the disease of addiction. Although I don't do this type of counseling now, I feel grateful to have touched the lives of those involved in such predicaments. It was definitely an eye opening experience for me.

I would like share some of what I have learned with the readers here to hopefully encourage whatever it they want to do with their lives.

- Write out your "WHY" and list the reasons behind wanting to make changes in your life and health.

- Work with a competent, compassionate, and proficient professional who can guide you through "HOW" to reach your goals. This professional can help you create a plan and work with you in order to help you stay on track and progress towards your goals.

- Sometimes when we have goals, we can stray from them. In these moments, remind yourself why you chose these goals instead of chastising yourself for falling short. It is important to remember we can always get back on our path to our goals and that it takes time to create new habits. Surrounding yourself with positive people and cheerleaders while communicating with the professional you chose to work with can also be helpful. It probably took several years to develop current habits and it's ok to ask for help and take time to create and implement new ones.

I hope you will all stop at nothing to go after what you see in your vision.

Shaweta "Shay" Vasudeva
www.ShayTheCoach.com
Telephone Number: 480-294-9953
E-mail Address: Shaythecoach@gmail.com

IGNITION 25

To Heal And Be Healed

Suzan Almushcab

Each of us on planet Earth has a unique blueprint of wisdom, talent, intelligence, love, and much more, and we thrive as a collective energy on all of that, vibrating eagerly to glide into the highest-existing emotional state of Bliss.

The goal for every one of us is to tap into his or her own deep-seated potential within the self, which allows it to unfold as we align with our passion and compassion of what we truly aspire to fulfill in reference to our driving motivation, focus, and purpose in life.

My ultimate purpose in life, and living that life to the fullest, is to create joy and be the joy itself, and to reflect it for those around me and globally. I envision this joy as I see it, feel it, and taste it, and manifest it by setting my goals toward this purpose. I find that all my thoughts and actions are driven toward this domain of Joy that is an absolute birthright of ours.

Joy to me is a state of being, it's a higher emotional level that embodies both energized health and true conscious happiness, which sprouts from within the self. It reflects and affects the quality of Life, of living Life with one's own sense of making reality and processing reality so that we make hope, desire, happiness, and impulse even more significant living directives that shape our lives.

My ultimate goal is to raise people's awareness and inspire them to create and access the perfect health and happiness from within themselves; hence, we can collectively inspire a healthy and a happy globe. I dream of lending my voice to achieving this end by speaking with clarity and passion that connects with people and helps in guiding them to find their true essence as they learn to love and nourish themselves.

We all have within reach the healing power that is needed to facilitate our mind and body to heal. We have learned from modern science and the ancient sages that our perception (our thoughts) often has a detrimental effect on our physical body. We also acknowledge that thoughts are energy, and this energy carries knowledge and information that can alter every cell in the body by having it either dance on a rhythm and feel happy or placing it under the pressure of stress hormones that result in an inflammatory effect on our body, which is manifested in disease or illness.

Today, as I write to inspire others, I'm seeking to align my goals toward my purpose, which is helping women who want to attain health and happiness from within. I am greatly aided in this quest by using the East Indian Healing system known as Ayurveda, which incorporated with neurolinguistic-programming tools, instructs them on how to unlearn the limiting beliefs and decisions that hold them back from realizing their full potential and creating what they wish to create. In addition, I offer a diet to balance their

Dosha (the principal force of energy) and energize them with a free dance.

As I coach women with this goal in mind, my plan is to help them unlock their potential as they go through the process of emotional healing. The positive energy of this experience encourages me to give even more help to others as I witness their feelings of liberation. Once this level of understanding is accomplished, they connect to their true essence and unleash their souls. In so doing, they shed all the contrived layers of expectations, beliefs, old stories, and outdated values that are weighing them down, and begin to rewrite their stories and re-create their reality by living in the moment and visualizing the bright prospects the future holds.

I have been on a learning journey all my life and I now know that I am the cause of everything that has happened in my life. This understanding comes with no resentment or regrets but rather with the acknowledgment, acceptance, and appreciation of the contrasts, conflicts, and indifferent circumstances that have gone into making my life as robust as it is today. I am becoming the being I am because embracing and learning from these various experiences have allowed me to become aligned with my source energy.

Remember that every new learning experience allows us to know what we don't know and to know that we don't know what we don't know. The process of learning prompts our brains to establish new networks of circuits and develop neuroplasticity. This leads to a richer comprehension of new experiences that can enhance the mind, especially if we keep revisiting and repeating the information learned. What we want to achieve is deprogramming the conditioning of our subconscious mind and reprogramming it with fresh knowledge as being the precursor of a new, more enlightened perspective.

My illness and the resulting unhappiness was due in part to my own lack of motivation and self-empowerment to heal myself from within. My journey of healing started by self-awakening and self-awareness after a lengthy bout of physical and life struggles. However, the process of learning from many mentors in my life, and even more so in the last four years, has transformed my life, allowed me to perceive and understand the meaning of the internal world and the meaning of one's own reality, and how we relate to others. Hence, the communication has been taken to a different domain, and life is experienced more fully with joy with my own reality being expressed in creating my desires as I deeply envision them.

My first lesson was the permaculture and the gateway to learning the Ayurvedic (East Indian ancient healing system) practice that integrates the body, mind, and soul focused on consciousness and the mind shift with the intent to make a change for self. However, this teaching inspired me to learn more about how our minds are conditioned from a young age and how limiting beliefs and decisions holds us back from the act of creating. So, I further pursued exploring the subconscious mind by learning the skills of Neurolinguistic programming. As I mentioned, I am on a journey of learning and self-discovery, and my brain cells are firing and re-wiring a new network, and I hope to keep inspiring others to strive to do the same. It's a decision and a choice we make on what we want to be and the personality and the personal reality we want to live.

Suzan Almushcab
www.suzymushcab.com
Suzy.mushcab@gmail.com
+1(587)969 7776

IGNITION 26

Survival On The Edge

Todd J. Speciale

I was born in upstate New York in a small town called Canandaigua. I only lived there for a short time in a small duplex until my parents finally moved us to Rochester. My father was in real estate and my mother used to run Brunswick bowling centers. We had a beautiful house on an acre of land in a great neighborhood. My brother and I and neighborhood children would play baseball and football in the yard, ride bikes and just literally be outside as often as we could. Back then there were no i-anything gadgets, so children enjoyed the luxury of the outdoors which I think is drastically be neglected these days. I was super competitive as a child. I never wanted to lose and always felt I could compete at anything, even though there was plenty I wasn't good at. I had this attitude of "its never good enough". At the age of eleven, the owner of my dad real estate company was arrested and his company was shut down for embezzling money. My father never knew and was mentally and financially devastated. My mother was the only one working when we found out and Brunswick had offered her a job in St. Louis Missouri.

There we barely made ends meet and my whilst dad also worked Mom's company was taken over a few times over. Whilst all this ensued over a few years, the love and light in our home never ran out because my parents loved each other and never let any situation get in the way of happiness in our home. But that bubble of happiness did burst when one day, mum received news of having cancer. All of us were devastated and the light and laughter left our home for quite a while as we watched Mom get more and more ill while she had treatments, lost her hair and went through the pain. She was a determined and strong woman and tried to be there for us no matter what. Dad was in and out of jobs but that too one day stopped and were living off coupons after a while. Dad was also very depressed and therefore very incapable of keeping our family afloat.

Instinct for survival kicked in and I went to work for my best friend's dad selling vacuum cleaners for $2000. He taught me a lot of tricks and thought i was very bad when I began I eventually got better and soon there was food on the table again and a decent place to live.

I soon discovered a pool hall and observed how things were done. I started gambling and became addicted to the lifestyle. I'd gamble away my school money and skip school to learn how to make money at the pool tables. İt wasn't long before I started making good money and I was so good at it that no one wanted to compete against me. By this time, I was shouldering all responsibilities for my family. One day I played a champion 9 ball hustler and lost all my savings to him. İ had ruined everything with just one game.

So, I quit gambling and started selling jewelry for a store called Hurst Fine Diamonds. I quickly started excelling and at age 20 was promoted to district sales manager. I knew how to talk to people, make them feel comfortable, negotiate, and close the deal. I started training in different locations in Missouri until one day I was scouted by Sterling jewelers and offered a district sales managers job for a large chain that owned thousands of jewelry stores. The job was in Orlando Florida and I took it. My whole family moved with me.

I worked long and hard hours barely seeing my wife and children although I was making 100k annually. Again, I started gambling, this time in poker. I took some challenges and started making more money than my regular job. It was an illegal way to earn a living but i was making great money and I continued. By this time my wife and I were divorced and I had a custody battle on my hands.

Reality crept in when one of my daughters asked me to come to school to talk about my job. That night I went to a poker game and negotiated my way into the timeshare business. I still continued running my card game business and was robbed several times. Once the robbery was bad enough to leave me with nothing except a bucket full of pennies.

I went into depression and started wasting my life playing X Box for hours every day. I would sleep long hours and eventually couldn't even feed my children properly. I had run out of money completely.

I took a job again, this time at Westgate and worked again I broke sales records. I immediately made a name for myself and started to realize that the money was AMAZING, but what I loved most was helping people that grew up in rough financial times like me, create a better future for them and their families. Showing people how to go from $30k a year to $100k a year. I loved sales training! I would have trainings and tell 10 people and 150 would show up! That was my drug. Watching people win, knowing I had a helping hand in it. This is what my future was.

I was doing well with motivation people through speaking and in 2016 I started writing, "The Things I Do Know." Although I was a fan of Les Brown and Grant Cardone I never did complete the book until my literally made me promise to complete it on his death bed. By this time, I was a certified Les Brown speaker and completed the book 30 days after my dad passed away.

The book became a best seller in 9 categories on Amazon. I held my first event with 300 seats sold out shortly after. İt feels like a life time of training but I'm just getting started with my life. Your story matters, always remember that but also remember to take your defining moments and make your dream come true. İt is possible.

Todd J. Speciale
Omnigroup Global
www.ToddSpeciale.com
www.OmnigroupGlobal.com
Todd@OmnigrouGlobal.com
407-810-8553

IGNITION 27

The Unsuspecting Call

Valerie Priester

My journey as a coach started with a simple request from five women who were my coworkers during my 13-year career as a Lead Project Manager.

The journey started with me becoming the leader of a Bible Study that we started on the job. For as far back as I can remember, I have always been the one selected to be the leader. It doesn't matter what type of group, organization, or gathering – I was always selected for leadership.

Our Bible study would meet every week for an hour. We would discuss topics that dealt with everyday living, including how to live the abundant life Jesus spoke about in the Bible. My vision for this study group was to teach others how to apply the biblical principles in their everyday life.

As the weeks went by, the participants of the study group grew more and more curious about how I was able to live my life in such a carefree and stress-free manner. Five women in the group made a request to work with me to help them deepen their relationship with God and live their full potential. I accepted their request because it has always been my nature to help others. Not only have I always been selected the leader, I have always been the person that my friends and family come to for sound advice.

I started working with these five women, helping them to identify with their greatness and understand their connection to God. In a matter of 3 short months, the lives of these women changed dramatically. One of the women decided to pursue her dream of owning a business, another woman started her journey of becoming a Realtor, and another woman became the leader of her women's ministry in a mega church. Marriages were reconciled, health journeys begun, and overall happiness filled their lives.

It was these five women that convinced me to explore the world of coaching. I had never heard of coaching except for sports coaching. They insisted that I had a special gift or talent to help people reach beyond their doubts and achieve massive change in their lives. I really didn't feel as though it was anything special because I simply was doing what I had always done and that was to encourage, uplift and motivate people to change.

After careful thought and prayer, I decided to explore the world of coaching. I searched for a school that would align with my beliefs and values. I found a school dedicated to Christian life coaching. I was clear that this school was where I needed to study because I would learn how to incorporate my faith-based beliefs into my coaching skills.

I completed my course work and received my certification. I decided to start my coaching business right away. My niche was women who wanted a deeper spiritual connection and understanding of their inner powers. I started my business part-time because I was still working a very stressful job as a Lead Project Manager. My first 3 years were spent trying to figure out how to find my clients. I would literally cry myself to sleep at night because I couldn't figure out how to market my business.

While I was on what seemed like a merry-go-round trying to figure out how to sustain a coaching business, I was somehow attracting people that needed my help. It wasn't many people but a few here and there. The advantage was that it helped me to sharpen my skills.

After a struggle I finally hired my first business coach. This decision changed things very quickly. Now I was clear on who I wanted to help. My message became clear and I began to attract more clients. I still wanted to help people with their mindset and spiritual connection, so I incorporated these teachings into my business coaching programs.

I went from helping women discover their inner power and spiritual connection to helping new heart-centered coaches build profitable businesses that they love. My spirituality helped in attracting the kind of clients that I needed and then I miraculously attracted prospective spiritual coaches also. It was nothing short of miraculous!

I recall resisting the idea from my business coach to focus on women coaches. It only took a few words from my coach to convince me to help those that were attracted to me.

I subsequently helped new coaches launch their businesses, get paying clients, and built their businesses in the way that they envisioned. My clients often tell me that it would not have been possible for them to reach the level of success they have without the coaching they receive from me. What I hear more than anything is that I helped them find their confidence to do the unbelievable. My daughter tells me that I am always an inspiration to her and her friends. I believe the way in which I help people the most is extracting the confidence that's already deep within.

I am asked all the time how I balance so many roles at one time. I have to share these ideas here:

- Start with your why and everything else will fall into place. Balance comes naturally when you do what you love

- Set clear boundaries for you and your family as you're on the journey of pursuing your dreams. I don't really believe in work/life balance. I believe it's more about prioritizing your life activities.

- Motivation comes from within. If your 'why' is important enough it should produce inner motivation to keep you in momentum. Never rely on outer influences to motivate you.

I pray that my story will inspire you to go after your dreams, live your purpose, and operate from your greatness.

Valerie Priester
www.valeriepriester.com
valeriep@victoriouslifecoaching.com
001-615-435-9249

12571528R00068

Made in the USA
Middletown, DE
16 November 2018